DRYDEN

AN ESSAY OF DRAMATIC POESY

DRYDEN

AN ESSAY OF DRAMATIC POESY

Edited with Notes
by
THOMAS ARNOLD

Third Edition, Revised
by
WILLIAM T. ARNOLD

ATLANTIC
PUBLISHERS & DISTRIBUTORS (P) LTD

Published by
ATLANTIC
PUBLISHERS & DISTRIBUTORS (P) LTD
7/22, Ansari Road, Darya Ganj, New Delhi-110002
Phones : +91-11-40775252, 23273880, 23275880, 23280451
Fax: +91-11-23285873
Web: www.atlanticbooks.com
E-mail: orders@atlanticbooks.com

Branch Office
5, Nallathambi Street, Wallajah Road, Chennai-600002
Phones : +91-44-64611085, 32413319
E-mail: chennai@atlanticbooks.com

Printed in India at Nice Printing Press, A-33/3A, Site-IV,
Industrial Area, Sahibabad, Ghaziabad, U.P.

PREFACE

It is interesting to note that the same cause—the great plague of 1665—which drove Milton from London to the Buckinghamshire village of Chalfont St. Giles, and there gave him leisure to complete the *Paradise Lost*, obliged Dryden also—the theatres being closed—to pass eighteen months in the country,—'probably at Charlton in Wiltshire,' says Malone,—where he turned his leisure to so good an account as, besides writing the 'Annus Mirabilis,' to compose in the following Essay the first piece of good modern English prose on which our literature can pride itself.

Charles II, having been much in Paris during his exile, had been captivated by the French drama, then in the powerful hands of Corneille and Molière. In that drama, when prose was not employed, the use of rhyme was an essential feature.

Dryden and others were not slow to consult the taste prevailing at Court. His first play, *The Wild Gallant*, was in prose; it is coarse and not much enlivened by wit, and it was not well received. In his next efforts Dryden took greater pains. He seems to have convinced himself that the attraction of rhyme was necessary to please the fastidious audiences for which he had to write; and after *The Rival Ladies*, of which a small part is in rhyme,—and *The Indian Queen* (1664), a play entirely rhymed, in which he assisted his brother-in-law Sir Robert Howard,—he brought out, early in 1665, his tragedy of *The Indian Emperor*, which, like *The Indian Queen*, is carefully rhymed throughout. In the enforced leisure which his residence at Charlton during the plague brought him, he thought over the whole subject, and this *Essay of Dramatic Posey* was the result.

In the course of time Dryden modified more or less the judgment in favour of rhyme which he had given in the *Essay.* In the prologue to the tragedy of *Aurungzebe, or the Great Mogul* (1675), he says that he finds it more difficult to please himself than his audience, and is inclined to damn his own play:—

> Not that it's worse than what before he writ,
> But he has now another taste of wit;
> And, to confess a truth, though out of time,
> Grows weary of his long-loved mistress, Rhyme.

Passion, he proceeds, is too fierce to be bound in fetters; and the sense of Shakespeare's unapproachable superiority,—Shakespeare, whose masterpieces dispense with rhyme,—inclines him to quit the stage altogether. Nevertheless his original contention,—however under the pressure of dejection, and the sense perhaps of flagging powers, he may afterwards have been willing to abondon it,—cannot be lightly set aside as either weak or unimportant; a point on which I shall have something to say presently.

Five critical questions are handled in the Essay, viz.—

1. The relative merits of ancient and modern poets.
2. Whether the existing French school of drama is superior or inferior to the English.
3. Whether the Elizabethan dramatists were in all points superior to those of Dryden's own time.
4. Whether plays are more perfect in proportion as they conform to the dramatic rules laid down by the ancients.
5. Whether the substitution of rhyme for blank verse in serious plays is an improvement.

The first point is considered in the remarks of Crites (Sir Robert Howard), with which the discussion opens. In connexion with it the speaker deals with the fourth point, assuming without proof that regard to the unities of Time and Place, inasmuch as it tends to heighten the illusion of reality, must place the authors who pay it above those who neglect it. Eugenius (Lord Buckhurst) answers him, pointing out the narrow range of the Greek drama, and several defects which its greatest admirers cannot deny. Crites makes a brief reply, and then Lisideius (Sir Charles Sedley) plunges into the second question, and ardently maintains that the French theatre, which was formerly inferior to ours, now,—since it had been ennobled by the rise of Corneille and his fellow-workers, —surpasses it and the rest of Europe. This commendation he grounds partly on their exact observance of the dramatic rules, partly on their exclusion of undue complication from their plots and general regard to the 'decorum of the stage,' partly also on the beauty of their rhyme. Neander (Dryden) takes up the defence of the English stage, and tries to show that it is superior to the French at every point. 'For the verse itself,' he says, 'we have English precedents of older date than any of Corneille's plays.' By 'verse' he means rhyme. He is not rash enough to quote *Gammer Gurton's Needle* and similar plays, with their hobbling twelve-syllable couplets, as 'precedents' earlier than the graceful French Alexandrines, but he urges that Shakespeare in his early plays has long rhyming passages, and that Jonson is not without them. At this point Eugenius breaks in with the question, whether Ben Jonson ought not to rank before all other writers, both French and English. Before undertaking to decide this point, Neander says that he will attempt to estimate the dramatic genius of Shakespeare, and of Beaumont and Fletcher. This he does, in an interesting and well-known passage (p.52). He then examines the genius of Jonson with reference to many special points, and gives an analysis of the plot of his comedy, *Epicoene, or The Silent Woman*; but he gives no direct answer to the question put by Eugenius. To the English stage as a whole he will not allow a position of inferiority; for 'our nation can never want in any age such who are able to dispute the empire of wit with any people in the universe' (p.60).

Crites now introduces the subject of rhyme, which he maintains to be unsuitable for serious plays. His argument, and Neander's answer, take up the rest of the Essay.

The personages who conduct the discussion are all of a social rank higher than that to which Dryden belonged. Sir Robert Howard, the son of the Earl of Berkshire, assumed the poet's lyre or the critic's stylus with an air of superiority which showed that he thought it a condescension in himself, a man of fashion, to associate with the poverty-stricken tribe of authors[n]. This tone is very noticeable in the Preface to *The Duke of Lerma*, which Dryden answered in his *Defence of the Essay*. Sir Charles Sedley[n] was a well-known Kentish baronet, and Lord Buckhurst, soon to be the Earl of Dorset, was heir to the illustrious house of Sackville. It is unlikely however that Dryden called himself 'Neander'[n] in the sense of 'novus homo,' a man of the people, desiring to rise above his station. Dryden was too proud of his own good birth for that, and the term appears to be a rough anagram on his own name, just as Lisideius was on that of Sedley.

This question as to the value of rhyme in dramatic poetry is by no means an obsolete or unprofitable inquiry; it still exercises our minds in the nineteenth century; it has received no permanent, no authoritative solution. It is usually assumed that Dryden was altogether wrong in preferring the heroic couplet to blank verse as the metre of serious dramas; and his own subsequent abandonment of rhyme—foreshadowed, as we have seen, in the prologue to *Aurung-zebe*—is regarded as an admission that his argument in favour of it was unsound. And yet much of what he says in defence of rhyme appears to be plain common sense and incontrovertible, and to deserve, whatever his later practice may have been, a careful consideration. After all, if the heroic rhyming plays of Dryden and Lee have found no successors, has not blank verse also notoriously failed, however able the hands which wielded it, to become the vehicle and instrument of an English dramatic school, worthy to be ranked alongside of the great Elizabethans? Since Dryden's, almost the only supremely excellent plays which English literature has produced are Sheridan's; and these are comedies, and in prose. Coleridge, Young, Addison, Byron, Shelley, Lytton-Bulwer,—all attempted tragedy in blank verse; and none of their tragedies can be said to live. The fact is, that the amazing superiority of Shakespeare, lying much more in the matter than in the form of his tragedies, makes us ready to admit at once that blank verse is the proper metre for an English tragedy because he used it. We do not see that the *ensemble* of the facts of the case,—viz. that no Elizabethan blank verse tragedy, *besides* those of Shakespeare, can be endured on the stage now, and that those of later dramatists have not been successful,—might lead us to the conclusion that Shakespeare triumphed rather *in spite* of blank verse than *because of* it.

Rhyme is merely one of the devices to which the poetic artist has recourse, for the purpose of making his work attractive and successful. Whether we take style, or metre, or quantity, or rhyme, the source of the pleasure seems to be always the same,—it lies in the victory of that which is formed over the formless, of the orderly over the anarchic,—in the substitution of Cosmos for Chaos,—in the felt contrast between the flat and bald converse of common life, and the measured and coloured speech of the orator or poet. Style belongs to prose, metre, quantity, and rhyme to poetry. Metre is the arrangement of the words and syllables of a composition into equal or equivalent lengths, the regular and expected recurrence of which is the source of a peculiar pleasure. Quantity is an improvement which can only have sprung up among those whose ears had long been trained in the strict observance of metre. By Quantity is meant the volume, or time, or weight of a syllable. A 'false quantity' consists in giving to a syllable a sound larger, longer, and heavier,—or on the other hand smaller, shorter, and lighter,—than that which the ear expects. It is obvious that constant study and observation would tend to determine the quantity of all syllables which it was possible to use in poetry; and not their natural quantity only, i.e. the weight which they had when standing alone, but also the quantity given them by their position before other syllables. This work of quantifying—as it may be called—after being carried to great perfection among the Greeks, was by them imparted to the Romans. Then it was that, 'horridus ille Defluxit numerus Saturnius,' the rough stumbling measure of Naevius and earlier poets went into disuse, and metre perfected by quantity, in the various moulds,—hexameter, elegiac, alcaic, &c.,—which Greek invention had created, took its place.

Crites rightly extols the metre and quantity of the ancients; his mistake is in inferring, because the ancients did not use rhyme, that therefore it should be eschewed by the moderns. Neander, or Dryden, states correctly enough that when Roman society was broken up, and the Latin tongue, upon the invasions of the Barbarians, had become corrupted into several vernacular dialects, whence gradually emerged the new languages of southern Europe, the niceties of quantity were obscured or forgotten, and some new attraction was felt to be necessary by the poetic artist in order to supply its place. This attraction was found in rhyme.

Attraction may however be studied too exclusively; there may be too much ornament as well as too little. Poetry, by presenting ideas in a beautiful dress, aims at making them loved. But the ideas themselves are the main consideration, and if the dress is too much obtruded,—if it attracts attention for its own sake and not for the sake of what it clothes, a fault is committed, and a failure incurred. As Aristotle considered (*Poet.* IV) that the elaborate Greek metres were unsuited for tragedy, and that the iambic trimeter, as 'nearer to common discourse,' was its proper instrument, so it is quite possible that in modern dramatic verse rhyme may fix the attention too much upon the *manner* of saying a thing, when the thing itself ought to concentrate upon it the thoughts and feelings of the spectators. But this extreme, owing to the difficulty and toil which finding rhymes imposes on the author, is less often met than its opposite. For one rhyming play which errs by excess of ornament, there are ten plays in blank verse which err by being flat and dull. Shakespeare in his best plays observes the true mean, making his blank verse so rhythmic and beautiful that the hearer requires no other ornament; while by rejecting rhyme he avoids the danger of weakening that interest which should be excited by the plot and the characters. When such blank verse as the following can be had, no one will ever ask for rhyme:—

> Forbear to sleep the night, and fast the day,
> Compare dead happiness with living woe;
> Think that thy babes were fairer than they were,
> And him that slew them fouler than he is;
> Bettering thy loss makes the bad causer worse;
> Revolving this will teach thee how to curse.

But when long passages are given us such as—

> There is no vice so simple but assumes
> Some mark of virtue on his outward parts:
> How many cowards, whose hearts are all as false
> As stairs of sand, wear yet upon their chins
> The beards of Hercules and frowning Mars,
> Who, inward search'd, have livers white as milk;
> And these assume but valour's excrement
> To render them redoubted, &c., &c.—

then, since the thoughts are neither supremely interesting in themselves, nor presented with supreme force or skill, the hearer is apt to grow weary, and to ask from the form of the verse that entertainment which he does not derive from the substance. In other words, he would, consciously or not, be glad of rhyme if he could get it.

There seems good reason to think that the French masterpieces of the seventeenth century would not, if they were not rhymed, hold their ground on the modern stage. With us, Shakespeare's genius enables us, even without the aid of rhyme, still to enjoy the acting of his plays; but this is true of no other dramatist of that age[1]. In his work on the Elizabethan dramatists, Charles Lamb produced passages from some of the best plays of all the principal authors; but it must be owned that they make no great impression. For this there are indeed other causes;—the wit is not such as amuses at the present day; the passion is rather Italian or Spanish than English;—but it is also true that the story is seldom sufficiently interesting, or the thoughts sufficiently striking, to enchain our attention for their own sakes, apart from the pleasure given by rhyme. On the other hand, in reading such a collection as Mr. Palgrave's *Golden Treasury*, all of us are conscious of the continued presence of pleasurable feeling. What reason can be found for this difference of impression, except that rhyme,—and often exquisitely managed rhyme,—is present throughout Mr. Palgrave's collection, and absent throughout Lamb's collection? If the English serious drama, expressed in blank verse, had continued to make progress from the beginning of the seventeenth century, and were in a flourishing condition at the present time, Dryden's plea for rhyme, since it might seem to have been disproved by the event, might well be rejected. But the English serious drama[2] at this moment is in such a low condition as to be almost non-existent. It seems therefore to be a question open to argument whether, in spite of the success,—due to exceptional power,—of *Hamlet* or *King Lear*, Dryden was not right in holding that the average dramatist could not safely dispense, if he wished permanently to please English audiences, with the music and the charm of rhyme.

The *Defence of the Essay of Dramatic Poesy* appeared later in the same year, 1668. After the publication of the Essay, Sir Robert Howard printed his tragedy of *The Duke of Lerma*, in

---

[1] Massinger's *New Way to pay Old Debts* is perhaps the only exception to the statment in the text.

[2] Of course I am not speaking of chamber pieces, but of plays intended for the stage. [Signs of revival are happily now visible—1901.]

the preface to which (printed by Malone in his collection edition of Dryden's prose works) he attacked with blundering vehemence the poet's argument on behalf of rhyme. Dryden seems to have been much nettled, and in this sharp and masterly reply he exposes the blunders, and makes short work of the arguments, of his brother-in-law. This *Defence* was prefixed to the second edition, just at that time called for, of *The Indian Emperor*. But Dryden must have been unwilling for many reasons to let this passage of arms ripen into a formal quarrel. From later editions of *The Indian Emperor* he suppressed the preface, and forbore ever to publish it in a separate form. It was not again printed till after his death.

Three editions of the *Essay of Dramatic Poesy* were published in the author's lifetime; see page1. Since 1700 it has been four times reprinted; first by Robert Urie in his *Select Essays on the Belles Lettres*, Glasgow, 1750; secondly, by Malone in his edition of Dryden's prose works (1800); thirdly, by Sir Walter Scott in his general edition of all Dryden's works, published in 1808[1]; and lastly, by Prof. W.P. Ker in his *Essays of John Dryden* (2 vols., 1900).

[1] Now republished under the superintendence of Mr. Saintsbury.

NOTE ON THE RHYMING PLAY

As the question is interesting and important, I subjoin to my father's views a catena of modern opinions on the subject.

W.T.A.

Rhyme has been so long banished from the theatre, that we know not its effects upon the passions of an audience; but it has this convenience, that sentences stand more independent on each other and striking passages are therefore easily selected and retained. Thus the description of Night in the *Indian Emperor*, and the rise and fall of empire in the *Conquest of Granada*, are more frequently repeated than any lines in *All for Love* or *Don Sebastian*.

JOHNSON, *Life of Dryden*.

The whole question of the use of rhyme in English drama has been persistently misunderstood, and its history misstated....The fashion of rhyme in the drama, then, to be exact, flourished from 1664 until Lee and Dryden returned to blank verse in 1678. Upon this it suddenly languished, and after being occasionally revived until the end of the century, found its last example in Sedley's *Beauty of the Conqueror*, published in 1702....During the first years of the Restoration, the principal playwrights were Porter, a sort of third-rate Brome; Killegrew, an imitator of Shirley; Stapylton, an apparently lunatic person; and Sir William Lower....Whenever these poetasters ventured into verse, they displayed such an incompetence as has never before or since disgraced any coterie of considerable writers. Their blank verse was simply inorganic, their serious dialogue a sort of insanity, their comedy a string of pot-house buffooneries and preposterous 'humours.' Dryden, in his *Wild Gallant*, and a very clever dramatist, Wilson, who never fulfilled his extraordinary promise, tried, in 1663, to revive the moribund body of comedy, but always in the style of Ben Jonson, and finally, in 1664, came the introduction of rhymed dramatic verse. For my own part, I frankly confess that I think it was the only course that it was possible to take. The blank iambics of the romantic dramatists had become so execrably weak and distended, the whole movement of dramatic verse had grown so flaccid, that a little restraint in the severe limits of rhyme was absolutely necessary.

E. GOSSE, *Seventeenth Century Studies*, p.236.

The intonation of English is not, like the intonation of French, such that rhyme is an absolute necessity to distinguish verse from prose; and where this necessity does not exist, rhyme must always appear to an intelligent critric a more or less impertinent intrusion in dramatic poetry. Indeed, the main thing which had for a time converted Dryden and others to the use of the couplet in drama was a curious notion that blank verse was too easy for long and dignified compositions. It was thought by others that the secret of it had been lost, and that the choice was practically between bad blank verse and good rhyme. In *All for Love*, Dryden very shortly showed *ambulando* that this notion was wholly groundless. From this time forward he was faithful to the model he had now adopted, and—which was of the greatest importance—he induced others to be faithful too. Had it not been for this, it is almost certain that *Venice Preserved* would have been in rhyme, that is to say that it would have been spoilt.

GEORGE SAINTSBURY, *Dryden* (English Men of Letters), p.57.

Le roi, qui avait vu notre tragédie francaise dans tout son éclat avec Corneille, avait rapporté en Angleterre la passion des idées francaises, et une grande difficulté à comprendre le théâtre différent de ce qu'il l'avait vu pendant ses années d'exil. 'Je viens,' écrivait le comte d'Orrery à un ami, 'de terminer une pièce dans le goût francais, parce que j'ai entendu le roi déclarer qu'il aimait mieux leur manière que la nôtre.' Ce qui l'avait surtout frappé dans notre tragédie, c'étaient les choses extérieures, comme l'unité de lieu, la dignité constante des personnages, et la rime. Le monarque, comme il est naturel, fit vite des adeptes, et son goût prévalut sans conteste, au grand préjudice du théâtre anglais. De l'unité de lieu il ne fut question que pour la forme, car elle ne ponvait guère s'accorder avec la nouvelle mise-en scène; mais on adopta la rime qui, si elle est nécessaire au rythme de nos vers francais, fait des vers anglais un chant lyrique insupportable dans un oeuvre de longue haleine, et qui est si manifestement contraire au génie dramatique de nos voisins, qu'elle n'avait jamais auparavant été employée sur leur théâtre et ne le fut jamais après.

BELJAME, *Le Public et les Hommes de lettres en Angleterre au XVIIIme Siècle*, p.40.

On peut porter un jugement analogue sur la versification lyrique de la 'comedia nueva.' C'est là une forme d'imitation qui nous paraît aujourd'hui fort étrange. Ce n'est pas que nous ayons la superstition de l'alexandrin. Mais il nous paraît invraisemblable qu'un monologue tragique accepte les contraintes d'un sonnet, et nous nous demandons si ce sont des héros de drame ou d'opéra qui échangent ainsi des dialogues de rédondilles. Prenons garde pourtant de n'être pas dupes d'une impression trop personnelle. Nous admettons sans peine que des personnages peints d'après nature s'expriment en vers. Cette extraordinaire convention en peut entraîner d'autres. Quand nous sommes familiarisés avec le lyrisme de Lope, nous trouvons de la grâce dans les effusions en mètres divers du 'galan' et de sa 'dama,' et nous ne nous plaignons pas que parfois des chants populaires retardent la marche de l'action. Si nous étions Espagnoles, peut-être penserions-nous comme l'auteur de l'*Arte Nuevo* qu'il faut des dizains pour exprimer des plaintes, que la romance ou les octaves conviennent seuls aux récits et que les amours demandent des quatrains, comme les graves réflexions des tercets. La variété des combinaisons rythmiques nous apparaîtrait comme une musique tour à tour passionnée et caressante, assez souple pour se renouveler avec les situations et les personnages. Mais nous ne sommes pas Espagnoles, et nous sommes assez désagréablement surpris par des strophes lyriques, au moment même où l'émotion allait être franchement tragique. Cette versification est peut-être utile à la *comedia*, mais elle est trop spéciale pour ne pas lui faire tort en pays étranger.

MARTINENCHE, *La Comedia Espagnole en France*, p.120.

The dispute about rhyming plays was decided as time went on, when Dryden came to discover that what had really attracted him in rhyme was something different from its suitability for dramatic purposes. The *Defence* contains one of his rather sad confessions of the uncogenial nature of some of the dramatic work he had to do. Comedy is not for him: 'I want that gaiety of humour which is required to it; my conversation is slow and dull, my humour saturnine and reserved.' For the other kind, for heroic drama in rhyme, he seemed to find more affinity in his genius. It is easy to see now, after *Absalom and Achitophel*, that it was the rhyme itself to which he felt himself drawn, rather than the heroic play.

W.P. KER, *Essays of John Dryden*, vol. I, Introduction, p.1.

The heroic play can be duly studied in the four independent works of Dryden: *The Indian Emperor, Tyrannic Love, or The Royal Martyr, The Conquest of Granada* (published 1676), and *Aureng-Zebe* (1676); in the State of Innocence, his version of Milton's version of the Fall; in the close of Otway's *Don Carlos*; and in the handling of the tale of Antony by Sir Charles Sedley (*Beauty the Conqueror*, 1677)....The polite public was prepared by its favourite reading to salute the heroic play. The grandiosity of Corneille's drama went for something, and the success of the Alexandrine may have helped to bribe the English poets into using the couplet....The couplet was, after all, a certain controlling force: it encouraged point. The blank verse that by degrees prevailed in our drama failed in control, and was prone to be extravagant, or weak, or both.

O. ELTON, *Augustan Ages*, pp.243-5.

In form French tragedy suggested the substitution of rime for blank-verse to Lord Orrery, 'the matchless Orinda,' and others, above all to Dryden, whose master-hand alone could have ensured even temporary success to so hopeless an experiment. For a time, with the support of the personal taste of King Charles II, the innovation maintained itself; when Dryden announced his intention to abandon it, the practice was doomed, and even before this we find it treated with undisguised ridicule by a leading comic dramatist[1]. There is no necessity in this place to refer to the arguments urged for and against it, which will be briefly noticed below. It proved impossible permanently to domesticate in English tragedy a form differing from that which had become proper to it, which it had adopted as its own, and the attempt to introduce rimed couplets into English comedy was even more transitory. But in truth these couplets, in the hands of Dryden and his followers, are something very different from the Alexandrines of Corneille, Racine, and Molière. The latter merely dignify and refine the style of polite conversation and courtly speech; the former not only modify expression, but may without exaggeration be said to change the tone of thought. It would not be easy to find any satisfactory reason for this difference in the nature of 'heroic' verse itself; for it was, of course, not antecedently necessary

[1] Wycherley, *The Plain Dealer*, Act ii, Sc. I (1674).

that this English metre should stereotype itself into the form elaborated in succession by Waller, Dryden, and Pope. But a poetic form, like a poetic species, cannot do violence to its history; and the English herioc couplet, when it came to be used by Dryden for the drama, had already grown radically unsuitable for such an application.

A.W. WARD, *History of Dramatic Literature*, iii, pp.316, 317.

...Dryden's defence of rime as an appropriate and desirable part of English tragic form has been definitively rejected in theory as well as abondoned in practice. As a matter of fact, already in Dryden's day rimed couplets had for English ears acquired a different sound from that which they possessed for French, partly because of the peculiar uses to which the practice of our dramatists (with variations indeed, but with a general steady tendency in the same direction) come to restrict them, partly from their constant employment in branches of poetry in which their effect was adverse to the semblance of continuity which is indispensable in dramatic dialogue. In the ears of English audiences, however much a passing fashion might endeavour to conceal the fact, they could not but constitute an impediment, instead of an aid, to dramatic illusion. The use of rime was therefore at variance with that definition of a play which Lisideius, with the approval of his interlocutors, gives in the *Essay*, and which requires it to be ' a just and lively image of human nature.'

Ibid., p.357.

When he (Milton) began to write blank verse, the blank verse of the dramatists, his contemporaries, was fast degenerating into more or less rhythmical prose. Suckling and Davenant and their fellows not only used the utmost licence of redundant syllables at the end of the line, but hustled and slurred the syllables in the middle till the line was a mere gabble, and interspersed broken lines so plentifully that it became impossible even for the most attentive ear to follow the metre....The history of blank verse reflects with curious exactness the phases of the history of the drama. When the metre was first set on the stage, in the Senecan drama, it was stiff and slow-moving; each line was monotonously accented, and divided from the next by so heavy a stress that the absence of rhyme seemed a wilful injury done to the ear. Such as it was, it suited the solemn moral platitudes that it was called upon to utter. Peele, Marlowe, and Shakespeare made the drama lyrical in theme and treatment; the measure, adapting itself to the change, became lyrical in their hands. As the drama grew in scope and power, addressing itself to a greater diversity of matter, and coming to closer grips with the realities of life, the lyrical strain was lost, and blank verse was stretched and loosened and made elastic. During the twenty years of Shakespeare's dramatic activity, from being lyrical it tended more and more to become conversational in Comedy, and in Tragedy to depend for its effects rather on the rhetorical rise and fall of the period than on the unit of the line. From the drama of Charles the First's time, when inferior workmen had carried these licences to the verge of confusion, it is a perfectly natural transition to the heroic couplet for Tragedy and the well-bred prose of Etherege for Comedy. Blank verse had lost its character; it had to be made vertebrate to support the modish extravagances of the heroic plays; and this was done by the addition of rhyme. Comedy, on the other hand, was tending already, long before the civil troubles, to social satire, and the life-like representation of contemporary characters and manners, so that prose was its only effective instrument.

WALTER RALEIGH, *Milton*, p.190.

To the above conspectus of modern views on the general subject should be added Mr. Swinburne's *Study of Shakespeare*, pp.32-48. The whole of the passage should be read, but the following only can here be quoted:—

Shakespeare was naturally addicted to rhyme, though, if we put aside the Sonnets, we must admit that in rhyme he never did anything worth Marlow's *Hero and Leander*: he did not, like Marlow, see at once that it must be reserved for less active forms of poetry than the tragic drama....But in his very first plays, comic or tragic or historic, we can see the collision and conflict of the two influences; his evil angel, rhyme, yielding step by step and note by note to the strong advance of that better genius who came to lead him into the loftier path of Marlow. There is not a single passage in *Titus Andronicus* more Shakespearean than the magnificent quatrain of Tamora upon the eagle and the little birds; but the rest of the scene in which we come upon it, and the whole scene preceding, are in blank verse of more variety and vigour than we find in the baser parts of the play; and these, if any scenes, we may surely attribute to Shakespeare...In this play then (*First Part of Henry VI*), more decisively than in *Titus Andronicus*, we find Shakespeare at work (so to speak) with both hands—with his left hand at rhyme and his right hand at blank verse. The left is loth to forego the practice of its peculiar music; yet, as the action of the right grows freer and its touch grows stronger, it becomes more and more certain that the other must cease playing, under pain of producing mere discord and disturbance in the scheme of tragic harmony...The example afforded by the *Comedy of Errors* would suffice to show that rhyme, however inadequate for tragic use, is by no means a bad instrument for romantic comedy...What was highest as poetry in the *Comedy of Errors* was mainly in rhyme; all indeed, we might say, between the prelude spoken by Ægeon and the appearance, in the last scene, of his wife: in *Love's Labour's Lost*, what was highest was couched wholly in blank verse; in the *Two Gentlemen of Verona*, rhyme has fallen seemingly into abeyance.

It is perhaps not so certain as is generally assumed that the rhyming play is dead beyond recall. It is probably not wholly without significance that the two most *popular* (though debased) of English stage-forms—the pantomime and the burlesque—are both in rhyme. A man of genius may yet show what can be done with rhyme, and he is most likely to show it in the field suggested by Mr. Swinburne. When, in the prologue to the last of his rhyming tragedies (*Aureng-zebe*), Dryden confessed to weariness of rhyme, his reason was that 'Passion's too fierce to be in fetters bound,' and he was clearly thinking of tragedy. But in certain kinds of romantic comedy, the artificiality of effect produced by those fetters might conceivably be only a grace the more.

W.T.A.

PREFACE TO THIRD EDITION

My father was actually engaged upon the revision of this book at the time of his death (November, 1900), and his working-copy contains a number of 'n's' in the margin, over against the passages on which he intended to write new notes. Some, at all events, of those notes were actually written, but they have unfortunately not been found. In these circumstances I have done my best to carry out his intentions so far as I could divine them. My task has been a good deal facilitated by the appearance of Prof. W.P. Ker's scholarly edition of the *Essays of John Dryden* (2 vols., Clarendon Press, 1900), and I have also to acknowledge obligations to Dr. A.W. Ward, whose *History of English Dramatic Literature* has been constantly at my elbow, and who has moreover rendered to his late friend and kinsman the service of piety involved in his allowing me to consult him upon special points. Perhaps the most prominent feature of my revision is the copiousness of quotation from Corneille. In no other way did it seem possible to bring home to the reader the greatness of Dryden's debt—extending not only to ideas and arguments, but even phrases—to his French contemporary. It should be added that the *New English Dictionary*, which is now far advanced, and which, it is already evident, will considerably lighten the labours of future annotators on English classics, has been freely drawn upon. The longer of my own notes are printed in square brackets.

May, 1901. WILLIAM T. ARNOLD.

Epistle Dedicatory

TO THE ESSAY OF

DRAMATIC POESY[1]

To The Right Honourable

CHARLES, LORD BUCKHURST[2].[N]

MY LORD,

As I was lately reviewing my loose papers, amongst the rest I found this Essay, the writing of which, in this rude and indigested manner wherein your lordship now sees it, served as an amusement to me in the country, when the violence of the last plague[3] had driven me from the town. Seeing then our theatres shut up, I was engaged in these kind of thoughts with the same delight with which men think upon their absent mistresses. I

[1] A=edition of 1668. B=edition of 1684 (here, in the main, reprinted). C=edition of 1693.

[2] C has, 'Charles Earl of Dorset and Middlesex, Lord Chamberlain of their Majesties Houshold, Knight of the Most Noble Order of the Garter, &c.' Lord Buckhurst had become Earl of Dorset in 1677. It is hard to say why Dryden did not give him his proper title in the edition of 1684.

[3] The great plague of 1665 (Malone).

confess I find many things in this Discourse which I do not now approve; my judgment being not a little altered[1] since the writing of it; but whether[2] for the better or the worse, I know not: neither indeed is it much material, in an essay, where all I have said is problematical. For the way of writing plays in verse, which I have seemed to favour, I have, since that time, laid the practice of it aside, till I have more leisure, because I find it troublesome and slow. But I am no way altered from my opinion of it, at least with any reasons which have opposed it. For your lordship may easily observe, that none are very violent against it, but those who either have not attempted it, or who have succeded ill in their attempt. It is enough for me to have your lordship's example for my excuse in that little which I have done in it; and I am sure my adversaries can bring no such arguments against verse, as those with which[n] the fourth act of *Pompey*[n] will furnish me[3] in its defence. Yet, my lord, you must suffer me a little to complain of you, that you too soon withdraw from us a contentment, of which we expected the continuance, because you gave it us so early. It is a revolt, without occasion, from your party, where your merits had already raised you to the highest commands, and where you have not the excuse of other men, that you have been ill used, and therefore laid down arms[4]. I know no other quarrel you can have to verse, than that[5] which Spurina[n] had to his beauty, when he tore and mangled the features of his face, only[6] because they pleased too well the sight[7]. It was an honour which seemed to wait for you, to lead out a new colony of writers from the mother nation: and upon the first spreading of your ensigns, there had been many in a readiness to have followed so fortunate a leader; if not all, yet the better part of poets[8]:

—pars, indocili melior grege; mollis et exspes[9]
Inominata perprimat cubilia.[n]

---

[1] a little altered, A. [2] whither, A.
[3] as the fourth Act of *Pompey* will furnish me with, A.
[4] Armes, A. [5] then that, A. [6] onely, A. [7] the lookers on, A.
[8] Writers, A. [9] expes, A.

I am almost of opinion, that we should force you to accept of the command, as sometimes the Praetorian bands have compelled their captains to recieve the empire. The court, which is the best and surest judge of writing[n], has generally allowed[n] of verse; and in the town it has found favourers of wit and quality. As for your own particular, my lord, you have yet youth and time enough to give part of them[1] to the divertisement of the public, before you enter into the serious and more unpleasant business of the world. That which the French poet said of the temple of Love, may be as well applied to the temple of the Muses. The words, as near as I can remember them, were these:

Le jeune homme a mauvaise grace,
N'ayant pas adoré dans le Temple d'Amour;
Il faut qu'il entre; et pour le sage,
Si ce n'est pas son vrai[2] sejour,
C'est un gîte[3] sur son passage.[n]

I leave the words to work their effect upon your lordship in their own language, because no other can so well express the nobleness of the thought; and wish you may be soon called to bear a part in the affairs of the nation, where I know the world expects you, and wonders why you have been so long forgotten; there being no person amongst our young nobility, on whom the eyes of all men are so much bent. But in the mean time, your lordship may imitate the course of Nature, who gives us the flower before the fruit: that I may speak to you in the language of the muses, which I have taken from an excellent poem to the king:

As Nature, when she fruit designs[4], thinks fit
By beauteous blossoms to proceed to it;
And while she does accomplish all the spring,
Birds to her secret operations sing.[n]

I confess I have no greater reason, in addressing this Essay to

---

[1] of it, A. [2] Si ce nest son vray, A. [3] Ce'st un giste, A.
[4] designes, A.

your lordship, than that it might awaken in you the desire of writing something, in whatever kind it be, which might be an honour to our age and country. And methinks it might have the same effect on you, which Homer tells us the fight of the Greeks and Trojans before the fleet, had on the spirit of Achilles; who, though he had resolved not to engage[1], yet found a martial warmth to steal upon him at the sight of blows, the sound of trumpets, and the cries of fighting men.

For my own part, if, in treating of this subject, I sometimes dissent from the opinion of better wits, I declare it is not so much to combat their opinions, as to defend my own, which were first made publick.[n] Sometimes, like a scholar in a fencing-school, I put forth myself, and shew my own ill play, on purpose to be better taught. Sometimes I stand desperately to my arms, like the foot when deserted by their horse; not in hope to overcome, but only to yield on more honourable terms. And yet, my lord, this war of opinions, you well know, has fallen out among the writers of all ages, and sometimes betwixt friends. Only it has been prosecuted by some, like pedants, with violence of words, and managed by others like gentlemen, with candour and civility. Even Tully had a controversy with his dear Atticus; and in one of his Dialogues, makes him sustain the part of an enemy in philosophy, who, in his letters, is his confident[n] of state, and made privy to the most weighty affairs of the Roman senate. And the same respect which was paid by Tully to Atticus, we find returned to him afterwards by Caesar on a like occasion, who answering his book in praise of Cato, made it not so much his business to condemn Cato, as to praise Cicero.[n]

But that I may decline some part of the encounter with my adversaries, whom I am neither willing to combat, nor well able to resist; I will give your lordship the relation of a dispute betwixt some of our wits on the same subject[2], in which they did not only speak of plays in verse, but mingled, in the freedom of discourse, some things of the ancient, many of the modern, ways of writing;

[1] ingage, A. [2] upon this subject, A.

comparing those with these, and the wits of our nation with those of others: it is true[1], they differed in their opinions, as it is probable[2] they would: neither do I take upon me to reconcile, but to relate them; and that as Tacitus professes of himself, *sine studio partium, aut irâ*[3], without passion or interest; leaving your lordship to decide it in favour of which part you shall judge most reasonable, and withal, to pardon the many errors of

Your Lordship's

Most obedient humble servant,

JOHN DRYDEN.

[1] 'tis true, A. [2] 'tis probable, A.
[3] Tac. Ann.I.i; sine ira aut studio, quorum causas procul habeo

TO THE READER

The drift of the ensuing discourse was chiefly to vindicate the honour of our English writers, from the censure of those who unjustly prefer the French before them. This I intimate, lest any should think me so exceeding vain,[n] as to teach others an art which they understand much better than myself. But if this incorrect Essay, written in the country without the help of books or advice of friends, shall find any acceptance in the world, I promise to myself a better success of the Second Part, wherein I shall more fully treat of[1] the virtues and faults of the English poets, who have written either in this, the epick[2], or the lyrick[3] way[4].

---

[1] A *om.* I shall more fully treat of.

[2] Epique, A.

[3] Lyrique, A.

[4] A has, 'will be more fully treated of, and their several styles impartially imitated.'

An Essay

OF

DRAMATIC POESY[1]

It was that memorable day[2], in the first summer of the late war, when our navy engaged[3] the Dutch; a day wherein the two most mighty and best appointed fleets which any age had ever seen, dispute the command of the greater half of the globe, the commerce of nations, and the riches of the universe: while[4] these vast floating bodies, on either side, moved against each other in parallel lines, and our countrymen, under the happy conduct of his royal highness[5], went breaking, by little and little, into the line of the enemies; the noise of the cannon from both navies reached our ears about the city,[n] so that all men being alarmed with it, and in a dreadful suspense of the event, which they knew[6] was then deciding, every one went following the sound as his fancy led him; and leaving the town almost empty, some took towards the park, some cross the river, others down it; all seeking the noise in the depth of silence.

[1] Dramatick Poesie, A.

[2] June 3, 1665 (Malone).

[3] ingag'd, A.

[4] Universe. While, A.

[5] James, duke of York, afterwards James II (Malone).

[6] we knew, A.

Among the rest, it was the fortune of Eugenius, Crites, Lisideius, and Neander, to be in company together; three of them persons whom their wit and quality have made known to all the town; and whom I have chose to hide under these borrowed names, that they may not suffer by so ill a relation as I am going to make of their discourse.

2. Taking then a barge, which a servant of Lisideius had provided for them, they made haste to shoot the bridge, and left behind them that great fall of waters which hindered them from hearing what they desired: after which, having disengaged[1] themselves from many vessels which rode at anchor in the Thames, and almost blocked[2] up the passage towards Greenwich, they ordered the watermen to let fall their oars more gently; and then, every one favouring his own curiosity with a strict silence, it was not long ere they perceived the air to break[3] about them like the noise of distant thunder, or of swallows in a chimney: those little undulations of sound, though almost vanishing before they reached them, yet still seeming to retain somewhat of their first horrour, which they had betwixt the fleets. After[4] they had attentively listened till such time as the sound by little and little went from them, Eugenius, lifting up his head, and taking notice of it, was the first who congratulated to[n] the rest that happy omen of our nation's victory: adding, that[5] we had but this to desire in confirmation of it, that we might hear no more of that noise, which was now leaving the English coast. When the rest had concurred in the same opinion, Crites, a person of a sharp judgment, and somewhat too delicate a taste in wit, which the world have mistaken in him for ill-nature, said, smiling to us, that if the concernment of this battle[6] had not been so exceeding great, he could scarce have wished the victory at the price he knew he must pay for it, in being subject to the reading and hearing of so many ill verses as he was sure would be made on

[1] disingag'd, A.
[2] blockt, A.
[3] The Air to break, A.
[4] Fleets: after.
[5] A *om.*
[6] battel, A.

that subject. Adding[1], that no argument could scape some of those eternal rhymers, who watch a battle with more diligence than the ravens and birds of prey; and the worst of them surest to be first in upon the quarry: while the better able, either out of modesty writ not at all, or set that due value upon their poems, as to let them be often desired[2] and long expected. 'There[3] are some of those impertinent people of whom you speak[4],' answered Lisideius, 'who to my knowledge are already so provided, either way, that they can produce not only a panegyrick upon the victory, but, if need be, a funeral elegy on the duke; wherein, after[5] they have crowned his valour with many laurels, they will[6] at last deplore the odds under which he fell, concluding that his courage deserved a better destiny.' All the company smiled at the conceipt of Lisideius; but Crites, more eager than before, began to make particular exceptions against some writers, and said, the publick magistrate ought to send betimes to forbid them; and that it concerned the peace and quiet of all honest people, that ill poets should be as well silenced as seditious preachers.[n] 'In my opinion,' replied Eugenius, 'you pursue your point too far; for as to my own particular, I am so great a lover of poesy, that I could wish them all rewarded, who attempt but to do well; at least, I would not have them worse used than one of their brethren was by Sylla the Dictator[7]:—*Quem in concione vidimus* (says Tully,) *cum ei libellum malus poeta de populo subjecisset, quod epigramma in eum fecisset tantummodo alternis versibus longiusculis, statim ex iis rebus quas tunc*[8] *vendebat jubere ei praemium tribui, sub ea conditione ne quid postea scriberet.*'[n] 'I could wish with all my heart,' replied Crites, 'that many whom we know were as bountifully thanked upon the same condition,—that they would never trouble us again. For amongst others, I have a mortal apprehension of two poets[n], whom this

[1] upon it; adding, A. [2] call'd for. [3] expected ! there, A.
[4] people you speak of, A. [5] and after, A. [6] A *om.* they will.
[7] then [than] Sylla the Dictator did one of their brethren heretofore, A.
[8] quae tunc, A.

victory, with the help of both her wings, will never be able to escape.' ''Tis easy[1] to guess whom you intend,' said Lisideius; 'and without naming them, I ask you, if one of them does not perpetually pay us with clenches upon words, and a certain clownish kind of raillery? If now and then he does not offer at a catachresis[2][n] or Clevelandism[3][n], wresting and torturing a word into another meaning: in fine, if he be not one of those whom the French would call *un mauvais buffon*; one who is so much a well-willer to the satire, that he intends at least to spare[4] no man; and though he cannot strike a blow to hurt any, yet he ought[5] to be punished for the malice of the action, as our witches are justly hanged, because they think themselves to be such[6]; and suffer deservedly for believing they did mischief, because they meant it.' 'You have described him,' said Crites, 'so exactly, that I am afraid to come after you with my other extremity of poetry. He is one of those who, having had some advantage of education and converse, knows better than the other what a poet should be, but puts it into practice more unluckily than any man; his style and matter are every where alike: he is the most calm, peaceable writer you ever read: he never disquiets your passions with the least concernment, but still leaves you in as even a temper as he found you; he is a very leveller in poetry: he creeps along with ten little words in every line[7], and helps out his numbers with *For to*, and *Unto*, and all the pretty expletives he can find, till he drags them to the end of another line; while the sense is left tired half way behind it: he doubly starves all his verses, first for want of thought, and then of expression; his poetry neither has wit in it, nor seems to have it; like him in Martial:[n]

[1] escape; 'tis easie, A. [2] Catecresis, A.
[3] so A; Cleivelandism B, and edd. [4] he spares, A.
[5] yet ought, A. [6] think themselves so, A.
[7] This passage evidently furnished Pope with his well-known couplet in the ESSAY ON CRITICISM;

> 'While *expletives* their feeble aid do join,
> And *ten low words* oft *creep* in one dull line.'

(Malone.)

Pauper videri Cinna vult, et est pauper.

'He affects plainness, to cover his want of imagination: when he writes the serious way, the highest flight of his fancy is some miserable antithesis, or seeming contradiction; and in the comic he is still reaching at some thin conceit, the ghost of a jest, and that too flies before him, never to be caught; these swallows which we see before us on the Thames are the just resemblance of his wit: you may observe how near the water they stoop, how many proffers they make to dip, and yet how seldom they touch it; and when they do, it is but the surface: they skim over it but to catch a gnat, and then mount into the air and leave it.'

3. 'Well, gentlemen,' said Eugenius, 'you may speak your pleasure of these authors; but though I and some few more about the town may give you a peaceable hearing, yet assure yourselves, there are multitudes who would think you malicious and them injured: especially him whom you first described; he is the very Withers[n] of the city: they have bought more editions of his works than would serve to lay under all their pies at the lord mayor's Christmas. When his famous poem first came out in the year 1660, I have seen them reading it in the midst of 'Change time; nay so vehement they were at it, that they lost their bargain by the candles' ends[n]; but what will you say, if he has been received amongst great persons[1]? I can assure you he is, this day, the envy of one[2] who is lord in the art of quibbling; and who does not take it well, that any man should intrude so far into his province.' 'All I would wish,' replied Crites, 'is, that they who love his writings, may still admire him, and his fellow poet: *Qui Bavium non odit*[n], &c., is curse sufficient.' 'And farther,' added Lisideius, 'I believe there is no man who writes well, but would think he had hard measure[3], if their admires should praise anything of his: *Nam quos contemnimus, eorum quoque laudes contemnimus*.' 'There are so few who write well in this age,' says Crites, 'that methinks any praises should be welcome; they

[1] the great Ones, A. [2] of a great person, A.

[3] think himself very hardly dealt with, A.

neither rise to the dignity of the last age, nor to any of the ancients: and we may cry out of the writers of this time, with more reason than Petronius of his, *Pace vestrâ liceat dixisse, primi omnium eloquentiam perdidistis*:[n] you have debauched the true old poetry so far, that Nature, which is the soul of it, is not in any of your writings.'

4. 'If your quarrel,' said Eugenius, ' to those who now write, be grounded only on your reverence to antiquity, there is no man more ready to adore those great Greeks and Romans than I am: but on the other side, I cannot think so contemptibly of the age in which I live[1], or so dishonourably of my own country, as not to judge we equal the ancients in most kinds of poesy, and in some surpass them; neither know I any reason why I may not be as zealous for the reputation of our age, as we find the ancients themselves were in reference to those who lived before them. For you hear your Horace saying,

> *Indignor quidquam reprehendi, non quia crassè*
> *Compositum, illepidève putetur, sed quia nuper.*[n]

And after:

> *Si meliora dies, ut vina, poemata reddit,*
> *Scire velim, pretium chartis quotus arroget annus?*[n]

'But I see I am engaging in a wide dispute, where the arguments are not like to reach close on either side; for poesy is of so large an extent, and so many both of the ancients and moderns have done well in all kinds of it, that in citing one against the other, we shall take up more time this evening than each man's occasions[2] will allow him: therefore I would ask Crites to what part of poesy he would confine his arguments, and whether he would defend the general cause of the ancients against the moderns, or oppose any age of the moderns against this of ours?'

5. Crites, a little while considering upon this demand, told Eugenius, that if[3] he pleased, he would limit their dispute to

[1] the Age I live in, A. [2] so C; mans occasions, A, B.

[3] that he approv'd his Proposals, and if, A.

Dramatique Poesie[1]; in which he thought it not difficult to prove, either that the ancients were superior to the moderns, or the last age to this of ours.

Eugenius was somewhat surprised, when he heard Crites make choice of that subject. 'For ought I see,' said he, 'I have undertaken a harder province than I imagined; for though I never judged the plays of the Greek or Roman poets comparable to ours, yet, on the other side, those we now see acted come short of many which were written in the last age: but my comfort is, if we are overcome, it will be only by our own countrymen: and if we yield to them in this one part of poesy, we more surpass them in all the other: for in the epic or lyric way, it will be hard for them to shew us one such amongst them, as we have many now living, or who lately were[2]: they can produce nothing so courtly writ, or which expresses so much the conversation of a gentleman, as Sir John Suckling; nothing so even, sweet, and flowing, as Mr. Waller; nothing so majestic, so correct, as Sir John Denham; nothing so elevated, so copious, and full of spirit, as Mr. Cowley; as for the Italian, French, and Spanish plays, I can make it evident, that those who now write surpass them; and that the drama is wholly ours.'[n]

All of them were thus far of Eugenius his[n] opinion, that the sweetness of English verse was never understood or practised by our fathers; even Crites himself did not much oppose it: and every one was willing to acknowledge how much our poesy is improved by the happiness of some writers yet living; who first taught us to mould our thoughts into easy and significant words,—to retrench the superfluities of expression,—and to make our rime[3] so properly a part of the verse, that it should never mislead the sense, but itself be led and governed by it.

6. Eugenius was going to continue this discourse, when Lisideius told him that[4] it was necessary, before they proceeded

---

[1] so A and B; Dramatick Poesie,C.

[2] were so, A.

[3] so A and B; rhyme, C.

[4] A *om.*

further, to take a standing measure of their controversy; for how was it possible to be decided who writ the best plays, before we know what a play should be? But, this once agreed on by both parties, each might have recourse to it, either to prove his own advantages, or to discover the failings of his adversary.

He had no sooner said this, but all desired the favour of him to give the definition of a play; and they were the more importunate, because neither Aristotle, nor Horace, nor any other, who had writ[1] of that subject, had ever done it.

Lisideius, after some modest denials, at last confessed he had a rude notion of it; indeed, rather a description than a definition; but which served to guide him in his private thoughts, when he was to make a judgment of what others writ: that he concieved a play ought to be, *A just and lively image of human nature, representing its passions and humours, and the changes of fortune to which it is subject, for the delight and instruction of mankind.*

This definition, though Crites raised a logical objection against it—that it was only *a genere et fine*, and so not altogether perfect[n], was yet well received by the rest: and after they had given order to the watermen to turn their barge, and row softly, that they might take the cool of the evening in their return, Crites, being desired by the company to begin, spoke on behalf of the ancients, in this manner:—

'If confidence presage a victory, Eugenius, in his own opinion, has already triumphed over the ancients: nothing seems more easy to him, than to overcome those whom it is our greatest praise to have imitated well; for we do not only build upon their foundations[2], but by their models. Dramatic Poesy had time enough, reckoning from Thespis (who first invented it) to Aristophanes, to be born, to grow up, and to flourish in maturity. It has been observed of arts and sciences, that in one and the same century they have arrived to great[3] perfection;[n] and no wonder,

[1] who writ, A. [2] foundation, A.
[3] a great, A.

since every age has a kind of universal genius, which inclines those that live in it to some particular studies: the work then, being pushed on by many hands, must of necessity go forward.

'Is it not evident, in these last hundred years, when the study of philosophy[n] has been the business of all the Virtuosi[n] in Christendom, that almost a new nature has been revealed to us? That more errors of the School[n] have been detected, more useful experiments in philosophy have been made, more noble secrets in optics, medicine, anatomy, astronomy, discovered, than in all those credulous and doting ages from Aristotle to us?—so true it is, that nothing spreads more fast than science, when rightly and generally cultivated.

'Add to this, the more than common emulation that was in those times of writing well; which though it be found in all ages and all persons that pretend to the same reputation, yet poesy, being then in more esteem than now it is, had greater honours decreed to the professors of it, and consequently the rivalship was more high between them; they had judges ordained to decide their merit, and prizes to reward it; and historians have been diligent to record of Eschylus, Euripides, Sophocles, Lycophron, and the rest of them, both who they were that vanquished in these wars of the theatre, and how often they were crowned: while the Asian kings and Grecian commonwealths scarce afforded them a nobler subject than the unmanly luxuries of a debauched court, or giddy intrigues of a factious city:—*Alit æmulatio ingenia*, (says Paterculus,) *et nunc invidia, nunc admiratio incitationem accendit*:[n] Emulation is the spur of wit; and sometimes envy, sometimes admiration, quickens our endeavours.

'But now, since the rewards of honour are taken away, that virtuous emulation is turned into direct malice; yet so slothful, that it contents itself to condemn and cry down others, without attempting to do better: it is[1] a reputation too unprofitable, to

[1] 'tis, A.

take the necessary pains for it; yet, wishing they had it, that desire[1] is incitement enough to hinder others from it. And this, in short, Eugenius, is the reason why you have now so few good poets, and so many severe judges. Certainly, to imitate the ancients well, much labour and long study is required; which pains, I have already shewn, our poets would want encouragement to take, if yet they had ability to go through the work[2]. Those ancients have been faithful imitators and wise observers of that nature which is so torn and ill represented in our plays; they have handed down to us a perfect resemblance of her; which we, like ill copiers, neglecting to look on, have rendered monstrous, and disfigured. But, that you may know how much you are indebted to those your masters, and be ashamed to have so ill requited them, I must remember you[n], that all the rules by which we practise the drama at this day, (either such as relate to the justness and symmetry of the plot, or the episodical ornaments, such as descriptions, narrations, and other beauties, which are not essential to the play[3],) were delivered to us from the observations which Aristotle made, of those poets, who either lived before him, or were his contemporaries: we have added nothing of our own, except we have the confidence to say our wit is better; of which, none boast in this our age, but such as understand not theirs. Of that book which Aristole has left us, περὶ τZς ΠοιητικZς, Horace his Art of Poetry is an excellent comment, and , I believe, restores to us that Second Book of his concerning Comedy, which is wanting in him.[n]

'Out of these two have[4] been extracted the famous Rules, which the French call *Des Trois Unites*, or, The Three Unities[n], which ought to be observed in every regular play; namely, of Time, Place, and Action.

'The unity of time they comprehend in twenty-four hours, the compass of a natural day, or as near as it can be contrived; and the reason of it is obvious to every one,—that the time of the

[2] A *om.* that desire.
[2] through with it, A.
[3] no brackets in A.
[4] has, A.

feigned action, or fable of the play, should be proportioned as near as can be to the duration of that time in which it is represented: since therefore, all plays are acted on the theatre in the space of time much within the compass of twenty-four hours, that play is to be thought the nearest imitation of nature, whose plot or action is confined within that time; and, by the same rule which concludes this general proportion of time, it follows, that all the parts of it are (as near as may be[1]) to be equally subdivided; namely[2], that one act take not up the supposed time of half a day, which is out of proportion to the rest; since the other four are then to be straitened within the compass of the remaining half: for it is unnatural that one act, which being spoke or written is not longer than the rest, should be supposed longer by the audience; it is therefore the poet's duty, to take care that no act should be imagined to exceed the time in which it is represented on the stage; and that the intervals and inequalities of time be supposed to fall out between the acts.

'This rule of time, how well it has been observed by the ancients, most of their plays will witness; you see them in their tragedies, (wherein to follow this rule, is certainly most difficult,) from the very beginning of their plays, falling close into that part of the story which they intend for the action or principal object of it, leaving the former part to be delivered by narration: so that they set the audience, as it were, at the post where the race is to be concluded; and, saving them the tedious expectation of seeing the poet set out and ride the begining of the course, they suffer you not to behold him[3], till he is in sight of the goal, and just upon you.

'For the second unity, which is that of Place, the ancients meant by it, that the scene ought to be continued through the play, in the same place where it was laid in the begining: for, the stage on which it is represented being but one and the same place, it is unnatural to conceive it many,—and those far distant

[1] A *om.* as near as may be.

[2] as namely, A.

[3] you behold him not, A.

from one another. I will not deny but, by the variation of painted scenes, the fancy, which in these cases will contribute to its own deceit, may sometimes imagine it several places, with some appearance of probability; yet it still carries the greater likelihood of truth, if those places be supposed so near each other, as in the same town or city; which may all be comprehended under the larger denomination of one place; for a greater distance will bear no proportion to the shortness of time which is allotted, in the acting, to pass from one of them to another; for the observation of this, next to the ancients, the French are to be most commended. They tie themselves so strictly to the unity of place, that you never see in any of their plays, a scene changed in the middle of an act: if the act begins in a garden, a street, or chamber, 'tis ended in the same place; and that you may know it to be the same, the stage is so supplied with persons, that it is never empty all the time: he who enters second[1], has business with him who was on before; and before the second quits the stage, a third appears who has business with him. This Corneille[2] calls *la liaison des scenes*[n], the continuity or joining of the scenes; and 'tis a good mark of a well-contrived play, when all the persons are know to each other, and every one of them has some affairs with all the rest.

'As for the third unity, which is that of Action, the ancients meant no other by it than what the logicians do by their *finis*, the end or scope of any action; that which is the first in intention, and last in execution: now the poet is to aim at one great and complete action, to the carrying on of which all things in his play, even the very obstacles, are to be subservient; and the reason of this is as evident as any of the former. For two actions, equally laboured and driven on by the writer, would destroy the unity of the poem; it would be no longer one play, but two: not but that there may be many actions in a play, as Ben Johnson has observed in his *Discoveries*[n]; but they must be all subservient to the great one, which our language happily expresses in the name

[1] that enters the second, A. [2] Corneil, A.

of *under-plots*: such as in Terence's *Eunuch* is the difference and reconcilement of Thais and Phædria, which is not the chief business of the play, but promotes the marriage of Chærea and Chremes's sister, principally intended by the poet. There ought to be but one action, says Corneille[n], that is, one complete action, which leaves the mind of the audience in a full repose; but this cannot be brought to pass but by many other imperfect actions, which conduce to it, and hold the audience in a delightful suspence of what will be.

'If by these rules (to omit many other drawn from the precepts and practice of the ancients) we should judge our modern plays, 'tis probable that few of them would endure the trial: that which should be the business of a day, takes up in some of them an age; instead of one action, they are the epitomes of a man's life; and for one spot of ground, which the stage should represent, we are sometimes in more countries than the map can shew us.

'But if we allow the Ancients to have contrived well, we must acknowledge them to have written[1] better. Questionless we are deprived of a great stock of wit in the loss of Menander among the Greek poets, and of Cæcilius, Afranius, and Varius, among the Romans; we may guess at Menander's excellency by the plays of Terence, who translated some of his[2]; and yet wanted so much of him, that he was called by C. Cæsar the half-Menander[n]; and may judge[3] of Varius[n], by the testimonies of Horace, Martial, and Velleius Paterculus. 'Tis probable that these, could they be recovered, would decide the controversy; but so long as Aristophanes and Plautus[4] are extant, while the tragedies of Euripides, Sophocles, and Seneca, are in our hands[5], I can never see one of those plays which are now written, but it increases my admiration of the ancients. And yet I must acknowledge further, that to admire them as we ought, we should understand them better than we do. Doubtless many things

[1] writ, A. [2] so A; B has 'them.' [3] A *om.* may judge.
[4] Aristophanes in the old Comedy and Plautus in the new, A.
[5] are to be had, A.

appear flat to us, the wit of which[1] depended on some custom or story, which never came to our knowledge; or perhaps on some criticism in their language, which being so long dead, and only remaining in their books, 'tis not possible they should make us understand[2] perfectly. To read Macrobius,[n] explaining the propriety and elegancy of many words in Virgil, which I had before passed over without consideration as common things, is enough to assure me that I ought to think the same of Terence; and that in the purity of his style (which Tully so much valued that he ever carried his works about him) there is yet left in him great room for admiration, if I knew but where to place it. In the mean time I must desire you to take notice, that the greatest man of the last age, Ben Johnson, was willing to give place to them in all things: he was not only a professed imitator of Horace, but a learned plagiary of all the others; you track him every where in their snow: if Horace, Lucan, Petronius Arbiter, Seneca, and Juvenal, had their own from him, there are few serious thoughts which are new in him: you will pardon me, therefore, if I presume he loved their fashion, when he wore their cloaths. But since I have otherwise a great veneration for him, and you, Eugenius, prefer him above all other poets,* I will use no farther argument to you than his example: I will produce before you Father Ben[3], dressed in all the ornaments and colours of the ancients; you will need no other guide to our party, if you follow him; and whether you consider the bad plays of our age, or regard the good plays[4] of the last, both the best and worst of the modern poets will equally instruct you to admire[5] the ancients.'

Crites had no sooner left speaking, but Eugenius, who had[6] waited with some impatience for it, thus began:

'I have observed in your speech, that the former part of it is

[1] whose wit, A. [2] know it, A.
[3] Father Ben to you, A. [4] good ones, A.
[5] esteem, A. [6] A *om.* had.

* See a high eulogy on Ben Jonson, by Lord Buckhurst (the Eugenius of this piece), written about the year 1668. Dryden's MISCEL. v.123, edit. 1716 (Malone).

convincing as to what the moderns have profited by the rules of the ancients; but in the latter you are careful to conceal how much they have excelled them; we own all the helps we have from them, and want neither veneration nor gratitude, while we acknowledge that, to overcome them, we must make use of the advantages we have received from them: but to these assistances we have joined our own industry; for, had we sat down with a dull imitation of them, we might then have lost somewhat of the old perfection, but never acquired any that was new. We draw not therefore after their lines, but those of nature; and having the life before us, besides the experience of all they knew, it is no wonder if we hit some airs and features which they have missed. I deny not what you urge of arts and sciences, that they have flourished in some ages more than others; but your instance in philosophy makes for me: for if natural causes be more known now than in the time of Aristotle, because more studied, it follows that poesy and other arts may, with the same pains, arrive still nearer to perfection; and, that granted, it will rest for you to prove that they wrought more perfect images of human life than we; which seeing in your discourse you have avoided to make good, it shall now be my task to show you some part of their defects, and some few excellencies of the moderns. And I think there is none among us can imagine I do it enviously, or with purpose to detract from them; for what interest of fame or profit can the living lose by the reputation of the dead? On the other side, it is a great truth which Velleius Paterculus affirms[n]: *Audita visis libentius laudamus; et præsentia invidia, præterita admiratione prosequimur; et his nos obrui, illis instrui credimus*: that praise or censure is certainly the most sincere, which unbribed posterity shall give us.

'Be pleased then in the first place to take notice, that the Greek poesy, which Crites has affirmed to have arrived to perfection in the reign of the old comedy, was so far from it, that the distinction of it into acts was not known to them; or if it were, it is yet so darkly delivered to us that we cannot make it out.

'All we know of it is, from the singing of their Chorus; and that too is so uncertain, that in some of their plays we have reason to conjecture they sung more than five times. Aristotle indeed divides the integral parts of a play into four. First, the *Protasis*[n], or entrance, which gives light only to the characters of the persons, and proceeds very little into any part of the action. Secondly, the *Epitasis*, or working up of the plot; where the play grows warmer, the design or action of it is drawing on, and you see something promising that it will come to pass. Thirdly, the *Catastasis*, called by the Romans, *Status*, the height and full growth of the play: we may call it properly the counter-turn[1][n], which destroys that expectation, imbroils the action in new difficulties, and leaves you far distant from that hope in which it found you; as you may have observed in a violent stream resisted by a narrow passage,—it runs round to an eddy, and carries back the waters with more swiftness than it brought them on. Lastly, the *Catastrophe*[n], which the Grecians called λύσις, the French *le denouement*, and we the discovery, or unravelling of the plot: there you see all things settling again upon their first foundations; and, the obstacles which hindered the design or action of the play once removed, it ends with that resemblance of truth and nature, that the audience are satisfied with the conduct of it. Thus this great man delivered to us the image of a play; and I must confess it is so lively, that from thence much light has been derived to the forming it more perfectly into acts and scenes: but what poet first limited to five the number of the acts, I know not; only we see it so firmly established in the time of Horace, that he gives it for a rule in comedy,—*Neu brevior quinto, neu sit productior actu.*[n] So that you see the Grecians cannot be said to have consummated this art; writing rather by entrances, than by acts, and having rather a general indigested notion of a play, than knowing how and where to bestow the particular graces of it.

'But since the Spaniards at this day allow but three acts, which they call *Jornadas*[n], to a play, and the Italians in many of theirs

[1] A has, 'Thirdly the Catastasis or Counterturn': the rest *om.*

follow them, when I condemn the ancients, I declare it is not altogether because they have not five acts to every play, but because they have not confined themselves to one certain number: it is building an house without a model; and when they succeeded in such undertakings, they ought to have sacrificed to Fortune, not to the Muses.

'Next, for the plot, which Aristotle called τὸ μνθὸς[n], and often τῶν πρᾷγμάτων σύνθεσις, and from him the Romans *Fabula*; it has already been judiciously observed by a late writer, that in their tragedies it was only some tale derived from Thebes or Troy, or at least something that happened in those two ages; which was worn so threadbare by the pens of all the epic poets, and even by tradition itself of the talkative Greeklings[n], (as Ben Johnson calls them,) that before it came upon the stage, it was already known to all the audience: and the people, so soon as ever they heard the name of Oedipus, knew as well as the poet, that he had killed his father by a mistake, and committed incest with his mother, before the play; that they were now to hear of a great plague, an oracle, and the ghost of Laius: so that they sat with a yawning kind of expectation, till he was to come with his eyes pulled out, and speak a hundred or more[1] verses in a tragic tone, in complaint of his misfortunes. But one Oedipus, Hercules, or Medea, had been tolerable: poor people, they escaped not so good cheap[n]; they had still the *chapon bouillé* set before them, till their appetites were cloyed with the same dish, and, the novelty being gone, the pleasure vanished; so that one main end of Dramatic Poesy in its definition, which was to cause delight, was of consequence destroyed.

'In their comedies, the Romans generally borrowed their plots from the Greek poets; and theirs was commonly a little girl stolen or wandered from her parents, brought back unknown to the city[2], there [falling into the hands of] some young fellow, who, by the help of his servant, cheats his father; and when her time comes, to cry[n],—*Juno Lucina, fer opem*,—one or other sees a

[1] hundred or two of, A. [2] the same city, A.

little box or cabinet which was carried away with her, and so discovers her to her friends, if some god do not prevent it, by coming down in a machine[n], and taking[1] the thanks of it to himself.

'By the plot you may guess much of the characters of the persons. An old father, who would willingly, before he dies, see his son well married; his debauched son, kind in his nature to his mistress[2], but miserably in want of money; a servant or slave, who has so much wit to strike in with him, and help to dupe his father; a braggadocio captain, a parasite, and a lady of pleasure.

'As for the poor honest maid, on whom the story is built, and who ought to be one of the principal actors in the play, she is commonly a mute in it: she has the breeding of the old Elizabeth way, which was[3] for maids to be seen and not to be heard; and it is enough you know she is willing to be married, when the fifth act requires it.

'These are plots built after the Italian mode of houses,—you see through them all at once: the characters are indeed the imitation of nature, but so narrow, as if they had imitated only an eye or an hand, and did not dare to venture on the lines of a face, or the proportion of a body.

'But in how strait a compass soever they have bounded their plots and characters, we will pass it by, if they have regularly pursued them, and perfectly observed those three unites of time, place, and action; the knowledge of which you say is derived to us from them. But in the first place give me leave to tell you, that the unity of place, however it might be practised by them, was never any of their rules: we neither find it in Aristotle, Horace, or any who have written of it, till in our age the French poets first made it a precept of the stage. The unity of time, even Terence himself, who was the best and most regular of them, has neglected: his *Heautontimorumenos*, or Self-Punisher, takes up visibly two days, says Scaliger[n]; the two first acts

---

[1] *take*, A. [2] so C; Mistres, B; Wench, A.

[3] A *om*. which was.

concluding the first day, the three last the day ensuing[1]; and Euripides, in tying himself to one day, has committed an absurdity never to be forgiven him; for in one of his tragedies[n] he has made Theseus go from Athens to Thebes, which was about forty English miles, under the walls of it to give battle, and appear victorious in the next act; and yet, from the time of his departure to the return of the Nuntius, who gives the relation of his victory, Æthra and the Chorus have but thirty-six verses; which[2] is not for every mile a verse.

'The like error is as evident in Terence his *Eunuch*, when Laches, the old man, enters by mistake into the house[3] of Thais; where, betwixt his exit and the entrance of Pythias, who comes to give ample relation of the disorders[4] he has raised within, Parmeno, who was left upon the stage, has not above five lines to speak. *C'est bein employer*[5] *un temps si court*, says the French poet[n], who furnished me with one of the observations: and almost all their tragedies will afford us examples of the like nature.

'It is true[6], they have kept the continuity, or, as you called it, *liaison des scenes*, somewhat better: two do not perpetually come in together, talk, and go out together; and other two succeed them, and do the same throughout the act, which the English call by the name of single scenes; but the reason is, because they have seldom above two or three scenes, properly so called, in every act; for it is to be accounted a new scene, not only every time[7] the stage is empty; but every person who enters, though to others, makes it so; because he introduces a new business. Now the plots of their plays being narrow, and the persons few, one of their acts was written in a less compass than one of our well-wrought scenes; and yet they are often deficient even in this.

[1] A has, 'therefore, sayes Scaliger, the two first acts concluding the first day were acted overnight; the three last on the ensuing day.'

[2] that, A.

[3] in a mistake the house, A.

[4] Garboyles, A.

[5] employé, A.

[6] 'Tis true, A.

[7] not every time, A.

To go no further than Terence; you find in the *Eunuch*, Antipho entering single in the midst of the third act, after Chremes and Pythias were gone off[n]; in the same play you have likewise Dorias beginning the fourth act alone; and after she had made a relation of what was done at the Soldier's[1] entertainment, (which by the way was very inartificial, because she was presumed to speak directly to the audience, and to acquaint them with what was necessary to be known, but yet should have been so contrived by the poet as to have been told by persons of the drama to one another, and so by them to have come to the knowledge of the people,) she quits the stage, and Phædria enters next, alone likewise: he also gives you an account of himself, and of his returning from the country, in monologue; to which unnatural way of narration Terence is subject in all his plays. In his *Adelphi*, or Brothers, Syrus and Demea enter after the scene was broken by the departure of Sostrata, Geta, and Canthara; and indeed you can scarce look into any of his comedies, where you will not presently discover the same interruption.

'But as they have failed both in laying of their plots, and in the management[2], swerving from the rules of their own art by misrepresenting nature to us, in which they have ill satisfied one intention of a play, which was delight; so in the instructive part they have erred worse: instead of punishing vice and rewarding virtue, they have often shewn a prosperous wickedness, and an unhappy piety: they have set before us a bloody image of revenge in Medea, and given her dragons to convey her safe from punishment; a Priam and Astyanax murdered, and Casandra ravished, and the lust and murder ending in the victory of him who acted them: in short, there is no indecorum in any of our modern plays, which if I would excuse, I could not shadow with some authority from the ancients.

'And one farther note of them let me leave you: tragedies and comedies were not writ then as they are now, promiscuously, by the same person; but he who found his genius bending to the

[1] Souldiers, A. [2] managing of 'em, A.

one, never attempted the other way. This is so plain, that I need not instance to you, that Aristophanes, Plautus, Terence, never any of them writ a tragedy; Æschylus, Euripides[n], Sophocles, and Seneca, never meddled with comedy: the sock and buskin were not worn by the same poet. Having then so much care to excel in one kind, very little is to be pardoned them, if they miscarried in it; and this would lead me to the consideration of their wit, had not Crites given me sufficient warning not to be too bold in my judgment of it; because, the languages being dead, and many of the customs and little accidents on which it depended lost to us, we are not competent judges of it. But though I grant that here and there we may miss the application of a proverb or a custom, yet a thing well said will be wit in all languages; and though it may lose something in the translation, yet to him who reads it in the original, 'tis still the same: he has an idea of its excellency, though it cannot pass from his mind into any other expression or words than those in which he finds it. When Phædria, in the *Eunuch*, had a command from his mistress to be absent two days, and, encouraging himself to go through with it, said, *Tandem ego non illa caream, si sit opus*[1], *vel totum triduum?*—Parmeno, to mock the softness of his master, lifting up his hands and eyes, cries out, as it were in admiration, *Hui! universum triduum!*[n] the elegancy of which *universum*, though it cannot be rendered in our language, yet leaves an impression on our souls: but this happens seldom in him; in Plautus oftener, who is infinitely too bold in his metaphors and coining words, out of which many times his wit is nothing; which questionless was one reason why Horace falls upon him so severely in those verses:

> *Sed proavi nostri Plautinos et numeros et*
> *Laudavere sales, nimium patienter utrumque,*
> *Ne dicam stolidè*[n].

For Horace himself was cautious to obtrude a new word on his

---

[1] si opus sit, A.

readers, and makes custom and common use the best measure of receiving it into our writings:

Multa renascentur quæ nunc [jam] cecidere, cadentque
Quæ nunc sunt in honore vocabula, si volet usus,
Quem penes arbitrium est, et jus, et norma loquendi[n].

The not observing this rule is that which the world has blamed in our satyrist, Cleveland[1] [n]: to express a thing hard and unnaturally, is his new way of elocution. 'Tis true, no poet but may sometimes use a catachresis[n]: Virgil does it—

Mistaque ridenti colocasia fundet acantho—[n]

in his eclogue of Pollio; and in his seventh Æneid,

mirantur et undæ,
Miratur nemus inssuetum fulgentia longe
Scuta virum fluvio pictasque innare carinas[n].

And Ovid once so modestly, that he asks leave to do it:

———*quem, si verbo audacia detur,*
Haud metuam summi dixisse Palatia cæli[n].

calling the court of Jupiter by the name of Augustus his palace; though in another place he is more bold, where he says,—*et longas visent Capitolia pompas*. But to do this always, and never be able to write a line without it, though it may be admired by some few pedants, will not pass upon those who know that wit is best conveyed to us in the most easy language; and is most to be admired when a great thought comes dressed in words so commonly received, that it is understood by the meanest apprehensions, as the best meat is the most easily digested: but we cannot read a verse of Cleveland's without making a face at it, as if every word were a pill to swallow: he gives us many times a hard nut to break our teeth, without a kernel for our pains. So that there is this difference betwixt his Satires and

[1] so A; Cleiveland,B.

doctor Donne's; that the one gives us deep thoughts in common language, though rough cadence; the other gives us common thoughts in abstruse words: 'tis true, in some places his wit is independent of his words, as in that of the *Rebel Scot*:

> *Had Cain been Scot, God would have chang'd his doom;*
> *Not forc'd him wander, but confin'd him home*[n].

Si sic omnia dixisset! [n] This is wit in all languages: it is like Mercury, never to be lost or killed:—and so that other—

> *For beauty, like white powder, makes no noise,*
> *And yet the silent hypocrite destroys*[n].

You see, the last line is highly metaphorical, but it is so soft and gentle, that it does not shock us as we read it.

'But, to return from whence I have digressed, to the consideration of the ancients' writing, and their wit; (of which by this time you will grant us in some measure to be fit judges.) Though I see many excellent thoughts in Seneca, yet he of them who had a genius most proper for the stage, was Ovid; he had a way of writing so fit to stir up a pleasing admiration and concernment, which are the objects of a tragedy, and to shew the various movements of a soul combating betwixt two different passions, that, had he lived in our age, or in his own could have writ with our advantages, no man but must have yielded to him; and therefore I am confident the *Medea* is none of his: for, though I esteem it for the gravity and sententiousness of it, which he himself concludes to be suitable to a tragedy,—*Omne genus scripti gravitate tragœdia vincit* [n],—yet it moves not my soul enough to judge that he, who in the epick way wrote things so near the drama as the story of Myrrha, of Caunus and Biblis, and the rest, should stir up no more concernment where he most endeavoured it[n]. The master-piece of Seneca I hold to be that scene in the *Troades*, where Ulysses is seeking for Astyanax to kill him: there you see the tenderness of a mother so represented in Andromache that it raises compassion to a high degree in the reader, and bears the nearest resemblance of any thing in the tragedies of the ancients[1] to the excellent scenes of passion in Shakspeare, or in Fletcher: for love-scenes, you will find few among them; their tragick poets dealt not with that soft passion, but with lust, cruelty, revenge, ambition, and those bloody actions they produced; which were more capable of raising horrour than compassion in an audience: leaving love untouched, whose gentleness would have tempered them; which is the most frequent of all the passions, and which, being the private concernment of every person, is soothed by viewing its own image in a publick entertainment.

'Among their comedies, we find a scene or two of tenderness, and that where you would least expect it, in Plautus; but to speak generally, their lovers say little, when they see each other, but *anima mea, vita mea*; Ζωὴ κᾷὶ ψνχZ^{n}, as the women in Juvenal's time used to cry out in the fury of their kindness[2]. Any sudden gust of passion (as an extasy of love in an unexpected meeting) cannot better be expressed than in a word and a sigh, breaking one another. Nature is dumb on such occasions; and to make her speak, would be to represent her unlike herself. But there are a thousand other concernments of lovers, as jealousies, complaints, contrivances, and the like, where not to open their minds at large to each other, were to be wanting to their own love, and to the expectation of the audience; who watch the movements of their minds, as much as the changes of their fortunes. For the imaging of the first is properly the work of a poet; the latter he borrows from[3] the historian.'

Eugenius was proceeding in that part of his discourse, when Crites interrupted him. 'I see,' said he, 'Eugenius and I are never like to have this question decided betwixt us; for he maintains, the moderns have acquired a new perfection in writing; I can only grant they have altered the mode of it. Homer

[1] their tragedies, A.

[2] kindness: then indeed to speak sense were an offence, A.

[3] of, A.

described his heroes men of great appetites, lovers of beef broiled upon the coals, and good fellows; contrary to the practice of the French Romances, whose heroes neither eat, nor drink, nor sleep, for love. Vigril makes Æneas a bold avower of his own virtues:

> *Sum pius Æneas, fama super æthera notus*[n]*;*

which, in the civility of our poets is the character of a fanfaron or Hector: for with us the knight takes occasion to walk out, or sleep, to avoid the vanity of telling his own story, which the trusty 'squire is ever to perform for him. So in their love-scenes, of which Eugenius spoke last, the ancients were more hearty, we more talkative: they writ love as it was then the mode to make it; and I will grant thus much to Eugenius, that perhaps one of their poets, had he lived in our age, *si foret hoc nostrum fato delapsus in ævum* [n], (as Horace says of Lucilius,) he had altered many things; not that they were not natural[1] before, but that he might accommodate himself to the age in which he lived[2]. Yet in the mean time, we are not to conclude any thing rashly against those great men, but preserve to them the dignity of masters, and give that honour to their memories, *quos Libitina sacravit* [n], part of which we expect may be paid to us in future times.'

This moderation of Crites, as it was pleasing to all the company, so it put an end to that dispute; which Eugenius, who seemed to have the better of the argument, would urge no farther: but Lisideius, after he had acknowledged himself of Eugenius his opinion concerning the ancients, yet told him, he had forborne, till his discourse were ended, to ask him why he preferred the English plays above those of other nations? and whether we ought not to submit our stage to the exactness of our next neighbours?

'Though,' said Eugenius, 'I am at all times ready to defend the honour of my country against the French, and to maintain, we are as well able to vanquish them with our pens, as our ancestors have been with their swords; yet, if you please,' added he, looking

[1] as natural, A. [2] age he liv'd in, A.

upon Neander, 'I will commit this cause to my friend's management; his opinion of our plays is the same with mine: and besides, there is no reason, that Crites and I, who have now left the stage, should re-enter so suddenly upon it; which is against the laws of comedy.'

'If the question had been stated,' replied Lisideius, ' who had writ best, the French or English, forty years ago, I should have been of your opinion, and adjudged the honour to our own nation; but since that time,' (said he, turning towards Neander,) ' we have been so long together bad Englishmen, that we had not leisure to be good poets. Beaumont, Fletcher, and Johnson, (who were only capable of bringing us to that degree of perfection which we have,) were just then leaving the world; as if in an age of so much horrour, wit, and those milder studies of humanity, had no farther business among us. But the Muses, who ever follow peace, went to plant in another country: it was then, that the great Cardinal of Richelieu began to take them into his protection; and that , by his encouragement, Corneille[n], and some other Frenchmen, reformed their theatre, (which before was as much below ours, as it now surpasses it and the rest of Europe). But because Crites in his discourse for the ancients has prevented me, by observing[1] many rules of the stage which the moderns have borrowed from them, I shall only, in short, demand of you, whether you are not convinced that of all nations the French have best observed them? In the unity of time you find them so scrupulous, that it yet remains a dispute among their poets, whether the artificial day of twelve hours, more or less, be not meant by Aristotle[n], rather than the natural one of twenty-four; and consequently, whether all plays ought not to be reduced into that compass. This I can testify, that in all their dramas writ within these last twenty years and upwards, I have not observed any that have extended the time to thirty hours: in the unity of place they are full as scrupulous; for many of their criticks limit it to that very spot of ground where the play is supposed to begin;

[1] touching upon, A.

none of them exceed the compass of the same town or city. The unity of action in all plays is yet more conspicuous; for they do not burden them with underplots, as the English do: which is the reason why many scenes of our tragi-comedies carry on a design that is nothing of kin to the main plot; and that we see two distinct webs in a play, like those in ill-wrought stuffs; and two actions, that is, two plays, carried on together, to the confounding of the audience; who, before they are warm in their concernments for one part, are diverted to another; and by that means espouse the interest of neither. From hence likewise it arises, that the one half of our actors are not known to the other. They keep their distances, as if they were Mountagues and Capulets, and seldom begin an acquaintance till the last scene of the fifth act, when they are all to meet upon the stage. There is no theatre in the world has any thing so absurd as the English tragi-comedy; 'tis a drama of our own invention[n], and the fashion of it is enough to proclaim it so; here a course of mirth, there another of sadness and passion, and a third of honour and a duel[1]: thus, in two hours and a half, we run through all the fits of Bedlam. The French affords you as much variety on the same day, but they do it not so unseasonably, or *mal à propos*, as we: our poets present you the play and the farce together; and our stages still retain somewhat of the original civility of the Red Bull[n]:

Atque ursum et pugiles media inter carmina poscunt[n].

The end of tragedies or serious plays, says Aristotle, is to beget admiration, compassion or concernment[n]; but are not mirth and compassion things incompatible? and is it not evident that the poet must of necessity destroy the former by intermingling of the latter? that is, he must ruin the sole end and object of his tragedy, to introduce somewhat that is forced into it[2], and is not of the body of it. Would you not think that physician mad, who, having prescribed a purge, should immediately order you to take restringents[3]?

[1] a third of Honour, and fourth a Duel, A.

[2] forced in, A. [3] restringents upon it, A.

'But to leave our plays, and return to theirs. I have noted one great advantage they have had in the plotting of their tragedies; that is, they are always grounded upon some known history: according to that of Horace, *Ex noto fictum carmen sequar* [n]; and in that they have so imitated the ancients, that they have surpassed them. For the ancients, as was observed before, took for the foundation of their plays some poetical fiction, such as under that consideration could move but little concernment in the audience, because they already knew the event of it. But the French goes farther:

> *Atque ita mentitur, sic veris falsa remiscet,*
> *Primo ne medium, medio ne discrepet imum*[n].

He so interweaves truth with probable fiction, that he puts a pleasing fallacy upon us; mends the intrigues of fate, and dispenses with the severity of history, to reward that virtue which has been rendered to us there unfortunate. Sometimes the story has left the success[n] so doubtful, that the writer is free, by the privilege of a poet, to take that which of two or more relations will best suit with his design: as for example, in[1] the death of Cyrus, whom Justin[n] and some other report to have perished in the Scythian war, but Xenophon affirms to have died in his bed of extreme old age[n]. Nay more, when the event is past dispute, even then we are willing to be decieved, and the poet, if he contrives it with appearance of truth, has all the audience of his party; at least during the time his play is acting: so naturally we are kind to virtue, when our own interest is not in question, that we take it up as the general concernment of mankind. On the other side, if you consider the historical plays of Shakspeare, they are rather so many chronicles of kings, or the business many times of thirty or forty years, or the business many times of thirty or forty years, cramped into a representation of two hours and an half; which is not to imitate or paint nature, but rather to draw her in miniature, to take her in little; to look upon her through the

[1] A *om.*

wrong end of a perspective, and receive her images not only much less, but infinitely more imperfect than the life: this, instead of making a play delightful, renders it ridiculous:—

Quodcunque ostendis mihi sic, incredulus odi [n].

For the spirit of man cannot be satisfied but with truth, or at least verisimility; and a poem is to contain, if not τὰ ἔτνμᾷ, yet ἐτύμοισιν ὁμοῖᾷ, as one of the Greek poets has expressed it[n].

'Another thing in which the French differ from us and from the Spaniards, is , that they do not embarrass, or cumber themselves with too much plot; they only represent so much of a story as will constitute one whole and great action sufficient for a play; we, who undertake more, do but multiply adventures: which, not being produced from one another, as effects from causes, but barely following, constitute many actions in the drama, and consequently make it many plays.

'But by pursuing closely[1] one argument, which is not cloyed with many turns, the French have gained more liberty for verse, in which they write; they have leisure to dwell on a subject which deserves it; and to represent the passions, (which we have acknowledged to be the poet's work,) without being hurried from one thing to another, as we are in the plays of Calderon, which we have seen lately upon our theatres, under the name of Spanish plots[n]. I have taken notice but of one tragedy of ours, whose plot has that uniformity and unity of design in it, which I have commended in the French; and that is *Rollo* [n], or rather, under the name of Rollo. The Story of Bassianus and Geta in Herodian: there indeed the plot is niether large nor inricate, but just enough to fill the minds of the audience, not to cloy them. Besides, you see it founded upon the truth of history,—only the time of the action is not reduceable to the strictness of the rules; and you see in some places a little farce mingled, which is below the dignity of the other parts; and in this all our poets are extremely peccant: even Ben Johnson himself, in *Sejanus* and *Catiline*,

[1] close, A.

has given us this oleo[n] of a play, this unnatural mixture of comedy and tragedy; which to me sounds just as ridiculously as the history of David with the merry humours of Golia's[1]. In *Sejanus* you may take notice of the scene betwixt Livia and the physician, which is a pleasant satire upon the artificial helps of beauty: in *Catiline* you may see the parliament of women; the little envies of them to one another; and all that passes betwixt Curio and Fulvia: scenes admirable in their kind, but of an ill mingle with the rest.

'But I return again to the French writers, who, as I have said, do not burden themselves too much with plot, which has been reproached to them by an ingenious person of our nation as a fault; for, he says, they commonly make but one person considerable in a play; they dwell on him, and his concernments, while the rest of the persons are only subservient to set him off. If he intends this by it,—that there is one person in the play who is of greater dignity than the rest, he must tax, not only theirs, but those of the ancients, and which he would be loth to do, the best of ours; for it is impossible but that one person must be more conspicuous in it than any other, and consequently the greatest share in the action must devolve on him. We see it so in the management of all affairs; even in the most equal aristocracy, the balance cannot be so justly poised, but some one will be superiour to the rest, either in parts, fortune, interest, or the consideration of some glorious exploit; which will reduce the greatest part of business into his hands.

'But, if he would have us to imagine, that in exalting one character the rest of them are neglected, and that all of them have not some share or other in the action of the play, I desire him to produce any of Corneille's tragedies, wherein every person, like so many servants in a well-governed family, has not some employment, and who is not necessary to the carrying on of the plot, or at least to your understanding it.

'There are indeed some protatick[n] persons in the ancients,

[1] Goliah's, C.

whom they make use of in their plays, either to hear or give the relation: but the French avoid this with great address, making their narrations only to, or by such, who are some way interessed[n] in the main design. And now I am speaking of relations, I cannot take a fitter opportunity to add this in favour of the French, that they often use them with better judgment and more *à propos* than the English do. Not that I commend narrations in general,—but there are two sorts of them. One, of those things which are antecedent to the play, and are related to make the conduct of it more clear to us. But 'tis a fault to choose such subjects for the stage as will force us on that rock, because we see they are seldom listened to by the audience, and that is many times the ruin of the play; for, being once let pass without attention, the audience can never recover themselves to understand the plot: and indeed it is somewhat unreasonable that they should be put to so much trouble, as that, to comprehend what passes in their sight, they must have recourse to what was done, perhaps, ten or twenty years ago[n].

'But there is another sort of relations, that is, of things happening in the action of the play, and supposed to be done behind the scenes; and this is many times both convenient and beautiful; for by it the French avoid the tumult to which we are subject[1] in England, by representing duels, battles, and the like; which renders our stage too like the theatres where they fight prizes[n]. For what is more ridiculous than to represent an army with a drum and five men behind it[n]; all which the hero of the other side is to drive in before him; or to see a duel fought, and one slain with two or three thrusts of the foils, which we know are so blunted, that we might give a man an hour to kill another in good earnest with them.

'I have observed that in all our tragedies, the audience cannot forbear laughing when the actors are to die; it is the most comick part of the whole play. All *passions* may be lively represented

[1] which we are subject to, A.

on the stage, if to the well-writing of them the actor supplies a good commanded voice, and limbs that move easily, and without stiffness; but there are many *actions* which can never be imitated to a just height: dying especially is a thing which none but a Roman gladiator could naturally perform on the stage, when he did not imitate or represent, but do it[1]; and therefore it is better to omit the representation of it.

'The words of a good writer, which describe it lively, will make a deeper impression of belief in us than all the actor can insinuate into us[2][n], when he seems to fall dead before us; as a poet in the description of a beautiful garden, or a meadow, will please our imagination more than the place itself can please our sight. When we see death represented, we are convinced it is but fiction; but when we hear it related, our eyes, the strongest witnesses, are wanting, which might have undeceived us; and we are all willing to favour the sleight, when the poet does not too grossly impose on us. They therefore who imagine these relations would make no concernment in the audience, are deceived, by confounding them with the other, which are of things antecedent to the play: those are made often in cold blood, as I may say, to the audience; but these are warmed with our concernments, which were before awakened in the play. What the philosophers say of motion, that, when it is once begun, it continues of itself, and will do so to eternity, without some stop put to it, is clearly true on this occasion: the soul, being already moved with the characters and fortunes of those imaginary persons, continues going of its own accord; and we are no more weary to hear what becomes of them when they are not on the stage, than we are to listen to the news of an absent mistress. But it is objected, that if one part of the play may be related, then why not all? I answer, some parts of the action are more fit to be represented, some to be related. Corneille says judiciously[n], that the poet is not obliged to expose to view all particular actions which conduce to the principal: he ought to select such of them to be seen, which will appear with

[1] naturally do it, A. [2] perswade us to, A.

the greatest beauty, either by the magnificence of the show, or the vehemence of passions which they produce, or some other charm which they have in them; and let the rest arrive to the audience by narration. 'Tis a great mistake in us to believe the French present no part of the action on the stage; every alteration or crossing of a design, every new-sprung passion, and turn of it, is a part of the action, and much the noblest, except we conceive nothing to be action till the players come[1] to blows; as if the painting of the hero's mind were not more properly the poet's work than the strength of his body. Nor does this anything contradict the opinion of Horace, where he tells us,

Segnius irritant animos demissa per aurem,
Quam quæ sunt oculis subjecta fidelibus.

For he says immediately after,

——————*Non tamen intus*
Digna geri promes in scenam; multaq; tolles
Ex oculis, quæ mox narret facundia præsens.

Among which many he recounts some:

Nec pueros coram populo Medea trucidet,
Aut in avem progne mutetur, Cadmus in anguem[n]*;* &c.

That is, those actions which by reason of their cruelty will cause aversion in us, or by reason of their impossibility, unbelief, ought either wholly to be avoided by a poet, or only delivered by narration. To which we may have leave to add, such as, to avoid tumult, (as was before hinted,) or to reduce the plot into a more reasonable compass of time, or for defect of beauty in them, are rather to be related than presented to the eye. Examples of all these kinds are frequent, not only among all the ancients, but in the best received of our English poets. We find Ben Johnson using them in his *Magnetick Lady* [n], where one comes out from dinner, and relates the quarrels and disorders of it, to save the

[1] they come, A.

undecent appearance of them on the stage, and to abbreviate the story; and this in express imitation of Terence, who had done the same before him in his *Eunuch*, where Pythias makes the like relation of what had happened within at the Soldiers[1] entertainment. The relations likewise of Sejanus's death, and the prodigies before it, are remarkable; the one of which was hid from sight, to avoid the horrour and tumult of the representation; the other, to shun the introducing of things impossible to be believed. In that excellent play, *The King and no King* [n], Fletcher goes yet farther; for the whole unravelling of the plot is done by narration in the fifth act, after the manner of the ancients; and it moves great concernment in the audience, though it be only a relation of what was done many years before the play. I could multiply other instances, but these are sufficient to prove that there is no errour in choosing a subject which requires this sort of narrations; in the ill management[2] of them, there may.

'But I find I have been too long in this discourse, since the French have many other excellencies not common to us; as that you never see any of their plays end with a conversion, or simple change of will[n], which is the ordinary way which our poets use to end theirs. It shews little art in the conclusion of a dramatick poem, when they who have hindered the felicity during the four acts, desist from it in the fifth, without some powerful cause to take them off their design[3]; and though I deny not but such reasons may be found, yet it is a path that is cautiously to be trod, and the poet is to be sure he convinces the audience that the motive is strong enough. As for example, the conversion of the Usurer in *The Scornful Lady* [n], seems to me a little forced; for, being an Usurer, which implies a lover of money to the highest degree of covetousness,—and such the poet has represented him,—the account he gives for the sudden change is, that he has been duped by the wild young fellow; which in reason might render him more wary another time, and make him punish himself

[1] Souldiers, A. [2] managing, A.

[3] A *om.* their design.

with harder fare and coarser clothes, to get up again what he had lost[1]: but that he should look on it as a judgment, and so repent, we may expect to hear[2] in a sermon, but I should never endure it in a play.

'I pass by this; neither will I insist on the care they take, that no person after his first entrance shall ever appear, but the business which brings him upon the stage shall be evident; which rule[3], if observed, must needs render all the events in the play more natural; for there you see the probability of every accident, in the cause that produced it; and that which appears chance in the play, will seem so reasonable to you, that you will there find it almost necessary: so that in the exit of the actor[4] you have a clear account of his[5] purpose and design in the next entrance; (though, if the scene be well wrought, the event will commonly deceive you;) for there is nothing so absurd, says Corneille, as for an actor to leave the stage, only because he has no more to say[n].

'I should now speak of the beauty of their rhyme, and the just reason I have to prefer that way of writing in tragedies before ours in blank verse; but because it is partly received by us, and therefore not altogether peculiar to them, I will say no more of it in relation to their plays. For our own, I doubt not but it will exceedingly beautify them; and I can see but one reason why it should not generally obtain, that is, because our poets write so ill in it. This indeed may prove a more prevailing argument than all others which are used to destroy it, and therefore I am only troubled when great and judicious poets, and those who are acknowledged such, have writ or spoke against it: as for others, they are to be answered by that one sentence of an ancient author:—*Sed ut primo ad consequendos eos quos priores ducimus, accendimur, ita ubi aut præteriri, aut æquari eos posse desperavimus, studium cum spe senescit: quod, scilicet,*

[1] to get it up again, A.
[2] hear of, A.
[3] A *om.* rule.
[4] exits of the Actors, A.
[5] their, A.

assequi non potest, sequi desinit;...prœteritoque eo in quo eminere non possumus, aliquid in quo nitamur, conquirimus[n]. '

Lisideius concluded in this manner; and Neander, after a little pause, thus answered him:

'I shall grant Lisideius, without much dispute, a great part of what he has urged against us; for I acknowledge that the French contrive their plots more regularly, and observe the laws of comedy, and decorum of the stage, (to speak generally,) with more exactness than the English. Farther, I deny not but he has taxed us justly in some irregularities of ours, which he has mentioned; yet, after all, I am of opinion that neither our faults nor their virtues are considerable enough to place them above us.

'For the lively imitation of nature being in the definition of a play, those which best fulfil that law ought to be esteemed superior to the others. 'Tis true, those beauties of the French poesy are such as will raise perfection higher where it is, but are not sufficient to give it where it is not: they are indeed the beauties of a statue, but not of a man, because not animated with the soul of poesy, which is imitation of humour and passions: and this Lisideius himself, or any other, however biassed to their party, cannot but acknowledge, if he will either compare the humours of our comedies, or the characters of our serious plays, with theirs. He who[1] will look upon theirs which have been written till these last ten years, or thereabouts, will find it an hard matter to pick out two or three passable humours amongst them. Corneille himself, their arch-poet, what has he produced except *The Liar* [n], and you know how it was cried up in France; but when it came upon the English stage, though well translated, and that part of Dorant acted to so much advantage[2] as I am confident it never received in its own country, the most favourable to it would not put it[3] in competition with many of Fletcher's or Ben Johnson's[n]. In the rest of Corneille's comedies you have little humour; he tells you himself, his way is, first to shew two

[1] He that, A. [2] A adds 'by Mr. Hart.' [3] A *om*.

lovers in good intelligence with each other; in the working up of the play to embroil them by some mistake, and in the latter end to clear it, and reconcile them[1].

'But of late years Moliere[2], the younger Corneille, Quinault, and some others, have been imitating afar off[3] the quick turns and graces of the English stage. They have mixed their serious plays with mirth, like our tragi-comedies, since the death of Cardinal Richelieu[n]; which Lisideius and many others not observing, have commended that in them for a virtue which they themselves no longer practise. Most of their new plays are, like some of ours, derived from the Spanish novels[n]. There is scarce one of them without a veil, and a trusty Diego, who drolls much after the rate of *The Adventures* [n]. But their humours, if I may grace them with that name, are so thin-sown, that never above one of them comes up in any play. I dare take upon me to find more variety of them in some one play of Ben Johnson's, than in all theirs together; as he who has seen *The Alchemist, The Silent Woman*, or *Bartholomew-Fair*, cannot but acknowledge with me.

'I grant the French have performed what was possible on the ground-work of the Spanish plays; what was pleasant before, they have made regular: but there is not above one good play to be writ on all those plots; they are too much alike to please often; which we need not the experience of our own stage to justify. As for their new way of mingling mirth with serious plot, I do not, with Lisideius, condemn the thing, though I cannot approve their manner of doing it. He tells us, we cannot so speedily recollect ourselves after a scene of great passion and concernment, as to pass to another of mirth and humour, and to enjoy it with any relish: but why should he imagine the soul of man more heavy than his senses? Does not the eye pass from an unpleasant object to a pleasant in a much shorter time than is required to this? and does not the unpleasantness of the first commend the beauty of the latter? The old rule of logick[n] might have convinced

[1] to clear it up, A. [2] de Moliere, A. [3] of afar off, A.

him, that contraries, when placed near, set off each other. A continued gravity keeps the spirit too much bent; we must refresh it sometimes, as we bait in a journey that we may go on with greater ease. A scene of mirth, mixed with tragedy, has the same effect upon us which our musick has betwixt the acts; which we find[1] a relief to us from the best plots and language of the stage, if the discourses have been long. I must therefore have stronger arguments, ere I am convinced that compassion and mirth in the same subject destroy each other; and in the mean time cannot but conclude, to the honour of our nation, that we have invented, increased, and perfected a more pleasant way of writing for the stage, than was ever known to the ancients or moderns of any nation, which is tragi-comedy.

'And this leads me to wonder why Lisideius and many others should cry up the barrenness of the French plots, above the variety and copiousness of the English. Their plots are single; they carry on one design, which is pushed forward by all the actors, every scene in the play contributing and moving towards it. Our plays[2], besides the main design, have under-plots or by-concernments, of less considerable persons and intrigues, which are carried on with the motion of the main plot: as[3] they say the orb of the fixed stars, and those of the planets, though they have motions of their own, are whirled about by the motion of the *primum mobile*, in which they are contained[n]. That similitude expresses much of the English stage; for if contrary motions may be found in nature to agree; if a planet can go east and west at the same time;—one way by virtue of his own motion, the other by the force of the first mover;—it will not be difficult to imagine how the under-plot, which is only different, not contrary to the great design, may naturally be conducted along with it.

'Eugenius has already shewn us, from the confession of the French poets, that the unity of action is sufficiently preserved, if all the imperfect actions of the play are conducing to the main

[1] and that we find, A. [2] Ours, A. [3] just as, A.

design; but when those petty intrigues of a play are so ill ordered, that they have no coherence with the other, I must grant that Lisideius has reason to tax that want of due connexion; for co-ordination in a play is as dangerous and unnatural as in a state. In the mean time he must acknowledge, our variety, if well ordered, will afford a greater pleasure to the audience.

'As for his other argument, that by pursuing one single theme they gain an advantage to express and work up the passions, I wish any example he could bring from them would make it good; for I confess their verses are to me the coldest I have ever read. Neither, indeed, is it possible for them, in the way they take, so to express passion, as that the effects of it should appear in the concernment of an audience, their speeches being so many declamations, which tire us with the length; so that instead of persuading us to grieve for their imaginary heroes, we are concerned for our own trouble, as we are in tedious[1] visits of bad company; we are in pain till they are gone. When the French stage came to be reformed by Cardinal Richelieu, those long harangues were introduced to comply with the gravity of a churchman. Look upon the *Cinna* and the *Pompey*; they are not so properly to be called plays, as long discourses of reason of state; and *Polyeucte* in matters of religion is as solemn as the long stops upon our organs[n]. Since that time it is grown into a custom, and their actors speak by the hour-glass, like our parsons[2];* nay, they account it the grace of their parts, and think themselves disparaged by the poet, if they may not twice or thrice in a play entertain the audience with a speech of an hundred lines[3]. I deny not but this may suit well enough with the French; for as we, who are a more sullen people, come to be diverted at our plays, so they, who are of an airy and gay temper, come thither to make themselves more serious: and this I conceive to

* Formerly an hour-glass was fixed on the pulpit in all our churches. (Malone.)

[1] the tedious, A. [2] as our Parsons do, A.

[3] an hundred or two hundred lines, A.

be one reason why comedies are[1] more pleasing to us, and tragedies to them. But to speak generally: it cannot be denied that short speeches and replies are more apt to move the passions and beget concernment in us, than the other; for it is unnatural for any one in a gust of passion to speak long together, or for another in the same condition to suffer him, without interruption. Grief and passion are like floods raised in little brooks by a sudden rain; they are quickly up; and if the concernment be poured unexpectedly in upon us, it overflows us: but a long sober shower gives them leisure to run out as they came in, without troubling the ordinary current. As for comedy, repartee is one of its chiefest graces; the greatest pleasure of the audience is a chace of wit[n], kept up on both sides, and swiftly managed. And this our forefathers, if not we, have had in Fletcher's plays, to a much higher degree of perfection than the French poets can reasonably hope to reach[2].

'There is another part of Lisideius his discourse, in which he has rather excused our neighbours, than commended them; that is, for aiming only to make one person considerable in their plays. 'Tis very true what he has urged, that one character in all plays, even without the poet's care, will have advantage of all the others; and that the design of the whole drama will chiefly depend on it. But this hinders not that there may be more shining characters in the play: many persons of a second magnitude, nay, some so very near, so almost equal to the first, that greatness may be opposed to greatness, and all the persons be made considerable, not only by their quality, but their action. 'Tis evident that the more the persons are, the greater will be the variety of the plot. If then the parts are managed so regularly, that the beauty of the whole be kept entire, and that the variety become not a perplexed and confused mass of accidents, you will find it infinitely pleasing to be led in a labyrinth of design, where you see some of your way before you, yet discern not the end till you arrive at it. And

[1] so C; Comedy's are, B; Comedy is, A.

[2] can arrive at, A.

that all this is practicable, I can produce for examples many of our English plays: as *The Maid's Tragedy, The Alchemist, The Silent Woman*: I was going to have named *The Fox* [n], but that the unity of design seems not exactly observed in it; for there appear[1] two actions in the play; the first naturally ending with the fourth act; the second forced from it in the fifth: which yet is the less to be condemned in him, because the disguise of Volpone, though it suited not with his character as a crafty or convetous person, agreed well enough with that of a voluptuary; and by it the poet gained the end at which he aym'd[2], the punishment of vice, and the reward of virtue, both[3] which that disguise produced. So that to judge equally of it, it was an excellent fifth act, but not so naturally proceeding from the former.

But to leave this, and pass to the latter part of Lisideius his discourse, which concerns relations: I must acknowledge with him, that the French have reason to hide[4] that part of the action which would occasion too much tumult on the stage, and to choose[5] rather to have it made known by narration to the audience. Farther, I think it very convenient, for the reasons he has given, that all incredible actions were removed; but, whether custom has so insinuated itself into our countrymen, or nature has so formed them to fierceness, I know not; but they will scarcely suffer combats and other objects of horrour to be taken from them. And indeed, the indecency of tumults is all which can be objected against fighting: for why may not our imagination as well suffer itself to be deluded with the probability of it, as with any other thing in the play? For my part, I can with as great ease persuade myself that the blows[6] are given in good earnest, as I can, that they who strike them are kings or princes, or those persons which they represent. For objects of incredibility,—I would be satisfied from Lisideius, whether we have any so removed from all appearance of truth, as are those of Corneille's

---

[1] appears, A.
[2] the end he aym'd at, A.
[3] A *om.* both.
[4] when they hide, A.
[5] and choose, A.
[6] the blowes which are struck, A.

Andromede [n]; a play which has been frequented the most of any he has writ. If the Perseus, or the son of an heathen god, the Pegasus, and the Monster, were not capable to choke a strong belief, let him blame any representation of ours hereafter. Those indeed were objects of delight; yet the reason is the same as to the probability: for he makes it not a Ballette[1] or masque, but a play, which is to resemble truth. But for death, that it ought not to be represented, I have, besides the arguments alledged by Lisideius, the authority of Ben Johnson, who has forborn it in his tragedies; for both the death of Sejanus and Catiline are related: though in the latter I cannot but observe one irregularity of that great poet; he has removed the scene in the same act from Rome to Catiline's army[n], and from thence again to Rome; and besides, has allowed a very inconsiderable time, after Catiline's speech, for the striking of the battle, and the return of Petreius, who is to relate the event of it to the senate: which I should not animadvert on him, who was otherwise a painful observer of τὸ πρέπον, or the *decorum* of the stage, if he had not used extreme severity in his judgment on the incomparable Shakespeare for the same fault[n].—To conclude on this subject of relations; if we are to be blamed for shewing too much of the action, the French are as faulty for discovering too little of it: a mean betwixt both should be observed by every judicious writer, so as the audience may neither be left unsatisfied by not seeing what is beautiful, or shocked by beholding what is either incredible or undecent.

'I hope I have already proved in this discourse, that though we are not altogether so punctual as the French, in observing the laws of comedy, yet our errours are so few, and little, and those things wherein we excel them so considerable, that we ought of right to be preferred before them. But what will Lisideius say, if they themselves acknowledge they are too strictly bounded[2] by those laws, for breaking which he has blamed the English? I will alledge Corneille's words, as I find them in the end of his Discourse of the three Unities:—*Il est facile aux speculatifs*

[1] Balette, C. [2] ti'd up, A.

d'estre sevères & c. "'Tis easy for speculative persons to judge severely; but if they would produce to publick view ten or twelve pieces of this nature, they would perhaps give more latitude to the rules than I have done, when, by experience, they had known how much we are limited[1] and constrained by them, and how many beauties of the stage they banished from it." To illustrate a little what he has said:—By their servile observations of the unities of time and place, and integrity of scenes, they have brought on themselves that dearth of plot, and narrowness of imagination, which may be observed in all their plays. How many beautiful accidents might naturally happen in two or three days, which cannot arrive with any probability in the compass of twenty-four hours? There is time to be allowed also for maturity of design, which, amongst great and prudent persons, such as are often represented in tragedy, cannot, with any likelihood of truth, be brought to pass at so short a warning. Farther; by tying themselves strictly to the unity of place, and unbroken scenes, they are forced many times to omit some beauties which cannot be shewn where the act began; but might, if the scene were interrupted, and the stage cleared for the persons to enter in another place; and therefore the French poets are often forced upon absurdities; for if the act begins in a chamber, all the persons in the play must have some business or other to come thither, or else they are not to be shewn that act; and sometimes their characters are very unfitting to appear there: as, suppose it were the king's bed-chamber; yet the meanest man in the tragedy must come and dispatch his business there, rather than in the lobby or courtyard, (which is fitter for him,) for fear the stage should be cleared, and the scenes broken. Many times they fall by it in a greater inconvenience; for they keep their scenes unbroken, and yet change the place; as in one of their newest plays[n], where the act begins in the street. There a gentleman is to meet his friend; he sees him with his man, coming out form his father's house; they talk together, and the first goes out: the second, who is a

[1] bound up, A.

lover, has made an appointment with his mistress; she appears at the window, and then we are to imagine the scene lies under it. This gentleman is called away, and leaves his servant with his mistress; presently her father is heard from within; the young lady is afraid the servingman should be discovered, and thrusts him into a place of safety[1], which is supposed to be her closet. After this, the father enters to the daughter, and now the scene is in a house; for he is seeking from one room to another for this poor Philipin, or French Diego[n], who is heard from within, drolling and breaking many a miserable conceit on the subject of his sad[2] condition. In this ridiculous manner the play goes forward[3], the stage being never empty all the while: so that the street, the window, the houses, and the closet, are made to walk about, and the persons to stand still. Now what, I beseech you, is more easy than to write a regular French play, or more difficult than to write an irregular English one, like those of Fletcher, or of Shakespeare?

'If they content themselves, as Corneille did, with some flat design, which, like an ill riddle, is found out ere it be half proposed, such plots we can make every way regular, as easily as they; but whenever they endeavour to rise to any quick turns and counterturns of plot, as some of them have attempted, since Corneille's plays have been less in vogue, you see they write as irregularly as we, though they cover it more speciously. Hence the reason is perspicuous, why no French plays, when translated, have, or ever can succeed on the English stage. For, if you consider the plots, our own are fuller of variety; if the writing, ours are more quick and fuller of spirit; and therefore 'tis a strange mistake in those who decry the way of writing plays in verse, as if the English therein imitated the French. We have borrowed nothing from them; our plots are weaved in English looms: we endeavour therein to follow the variety and greatness of characters which are derived to us from Shakespeare and

[1] for 'into a place of safety,' A has ' in through a door.'

[2] upon his sad, A.

[3] goes on, A.

Fletcher; the copiousness and well-knitting of the intrigues we have from Johnson; and for the verse itself we have English precedents of elder date than any of Corneille's plays. Not to name our old comedies before Shakspeare, which were all writ in verse of six feet, or Alexandrines[n], such as the French now use,—I can shew in Shakespeare, many scenes of rhyme together, and the like in Ben Jonhson's tragedies: in *Catiline* and *Sejanus* sometimes thirty or forty lines,—I mean besides the Chorus, or the monologues; which, by the way, shewed Ben no enemy to this way of writing, especially if you read[1] his *Sad Shepherd*[n], which goes sometimes on rhyme, sometines on blank verse, like an horse who eases himself on trot and amble. You find him likewise commending Fletcher's pastoral of *The Faithful Shepherdess*, which is for the most part rhyme, though not refined to that purity to which it hath since been brought. And these examples are enough to clear us from a servile imitation of the French.

'But to return whence[2][n] I have digressed: I dare boldly affirm these two things of the English drama;—First, that we have many plays of ours as regular as any of theirs, and which, besides, have more variety of plot and characters; and secondly, that in most of the irregular plays of Shakespeare or Fletcher, (for Ben Johnson's are for the most part regular,) there is a more masculine fancy and greater spirit in the writing, than there is in any of the French. I could produce, even in Shakespeare's and Fletcher's works, some plays which are almost exactly formed; as *The Merry Wives of Windsor*[n], and *The Scornful Lady*: but because (generally speaking) Shakespeare, who writ first, did not perfectly observe the laws of comedy, and Fletcher, who came nearer to perfection, yet through carelessness made many faults; I will take the pattern of a perfect play from Ben Johnson, who was a careful and learned observer of the dramatick laws, and from all his comedies I shall select *The Silent Woman*; of which I will make a short examen, according to those rules which the French observe.'

[1] look upon, A. [2] from whence, A.

As Neander was beginning to examine *The Silent Woman*, Eugenius, earnestly regarding him[1]; 'I beseech you, Neander,' said he, 'gratify the company, and me in particular, so far, as before you speak of the play, to give us a character of the author; and tell us frankly your opinion, whether you do not think all writers, both French and English, ought to give place to him.'

'I fear,' replied Neander, 'that in obeying your commands I shall draw some envy[2] on myself. Besides, in performing them, it will be first necessary to speak somewhat of Shakespeare and Fletcher, his rivals in poesy; and one of them, in my opinion, at least his equal, perhaps[n] his superior.

'To begin, then, with Shakespeare. He was the man who of all modern, and perhaps ancient poets, had the largest and most comprehensive soul. All the images of nature were still present to him, and he drew them, not laboriously, but luckily; when he describes any thing, you more than see it, you feel it too. Those who accuse him to have wanted learning, give him the greater commendation: he was naturally learned; he needed not the spectacles of books to read nature; he looked inwards, and found her there. I cannot say he is every where alike; were he so, I should do him injury to compare him with the greatest of mankind. He is many times flat, insipid; his comick wit degenerating into clenches, his serious swelling into bombast. But he is always great, when some great occasion is presented to him; no man can say he ever had a fit subject for his wit, and did not then raise himself as high above the rest of poets,

Quantum lenta solent inter viburna cupressi [n].

The consideration of this made Mr. Hales[n] of Eaton say, that there was no subject of which any poet ever writ, but he would produce it much better done[3] in Shakespeare; and however others are now generally preferred before him, yet the age wherein he

[1] looking earnestly upon him, A.
[2] a little envy, A. [3] treated of, A.

lived, which had contemporaries with him Fletcher and Johnson, never equalled them to him in their esteem: and in the last king's court, when Ben's reputation was at highest, Sir John Suckling, and with him the greater part of the courtiers, set our Shakespeare far above him.

'Beaumont and Fletcher, of whom I am next to speak, had, with the advantage of Shakspeare's wit, which was their precedent, great natural gifts, improved by study: Beaumont especially being so accurate a judge of plays, that Ben Johnson, while he lived, submitted all his writings to his censure, and, 'tis thought, used his judgment in correcting, if not contriving, all his plots. What value he had for him, appears by the verses he writ to him[n]; and therefore I need speak no farther of it. The first play that brought Fletcher and him in esteem was their *Philaster*[n]: for before that, they had written two or three very unsuccessfully, as the like is reported of Ben Johnson, before he writ *Every Man in his Humour*. Their plots were generally more regular than Shakespeare's, especially those which were made before Beaumont's death*; and they understood and imitated the conversation of gentlemen much better; whose wild debaucheries, and quickness of wit in reparties, no poets before them could paint[1] as they have done. Humour, which[2] Ben Johnson derived from particular persons, they made it not their business to describe: they represented all the passions very lively, but above all, love. I am apt to believe the English language in them

* Sir Aston Cokain long since complained, that the booksellers who, in 1647, published thirty-four plays under the names of Beaumont and Fletcher, had not ascertained how many of them were written solely by Fletcher:

> 'In the large book of plays you late did print,
> In Beaumont's and in Fletcher's name, why in't
> Did you not justice? give to each his due?
> For Beaumont of those many writ in few;
> And Massinger in other few: the main
> Being sole issues of sweet Fletcher's brain.' (Malone.)

[1] for 'before them could paint' A has 'can ever paint.'

[2] This Humour of which, A.

arrived to its highest perfection: what words have since been taken in, are rather superfluous than ornamental[1]. Their plays[n] are now the most pleasant and frequent entertainments of the stage; two of theirs being acted through the year for one of Shakspeare's or Johnson's: the reason is, because there is a certain gaiety in their comedies, and pathos in their more serious plays, which suits generally with all men's humours. Shakspeare's language is likewise a little obsolete, and Ben Johnson's wit comes short of theirs.

'As for Johnson, to whose character I am now arrived, if we look upon him while he was himself, (for his last plays were but his dotages[n],) I think him the most learned and judicious writer which any theatre ever had. He was a most severe judge of himself, as well as others. One cannot say he wanted wit, but rather that he was frugal of it. In his works you find little to retrench or alter. Wit, and language, and humour also in some measure, we had before him; but something of art was wanting to the drama, till he came. He managed his strength to more advantage than any who preceded him. You seldom find him making love in any of his scenes, or endeavouring to move the passions; his genius was too sullen and saturniine to do it gracefully, especially when he knew he came after those who had performed both to such an height. Humour was his proper sphere; and in that he delighted most to represent mechanick people. He was deeply conversant in the ancients, both Greek and Latin, and he borrowed boldly from them: there is scarce a poet or historian among the Roman authors of those times whom he has not translated in *Sejanus* and *Catiline*. But he has done his robberies so openly, that one may see he fears not to be taxed by any law. He invades authors like a monarch; and what would be theft in other poets, is only victory in him. With the spoils of these writers he so represents old Rome to us, in its rites, ceremonies, and customs, that if one of their poets had written either of his tragedies, we had seen less of it than in him. If there

[1] necessary, A.

was any fault in his language, 'twas that he weaved it too closely and laboriously, in his comedies especially[1]: perhaps too, he did a little too much Romanize our tongue, leaving the words which he translated almost as much Latin as he found them: wherein, though he learnedly followed their[2] language, he did not enough comply with the idiom of ours. If I would compare him with Shakespeare, I must acknowledge him the more correct poet, but Shakespeare the greater wit. Shakespeare was the Homer, or father of our dramatick poets; Johnson was the Virgil, the pattern of elaborate writing; I admire him, but I love Shakespeare. To conclude of him; as he has given us the most correct plays, so in the precepts which he has laid down in his *Discoveries* [n], we have as many and profitable rules for perfecting the stage, as any wherewith the French can furnish us.

'Having thus spoken of the author, I proceed to the examination of his comedy, *The Silent Woman* [n].

EXAMEN OF THE SILENT WOMAN.

'To begin first with the length of the action; it is so far from exceeding the compass of a natural day, that it takes not up an artificial one. 'Tis all included in the limits of three hours and an half, which is no more than is required for the presentment on the stage: a beauty perhaps not much observed; if it had, we should not have looked on the Spanish translation of *Five Hours** with so much wonder. The scene of it is laid in London; the latitude of place is almost as little as you can imagine; for it lies all within the compass of two houses, and after the first act, in one. The continuity of scenes is observed more than in any of our plays, except his own *Fox* and *Alchemist*. They are not broken above twice or thrice at most in the whole comedy; and in the two best of Corneille's plays, the *Cid* and *Cinna*, they are interrupted once[3]. The action of the play is entirely one; the end

[1] for 'comedies especially' A has 'serious Playes.'

[2] the idiom of their, A.

* See p.43

[3] once apiece, A.

or aim of which is the settling Morose's estate on Dauphine. The intrigue of it is the greatest and most noble of any pure unmixed comedy in any language; you see in it many persons of various characters and humours, and all delightful. As first, Morose, or an old man, to whom all noise but his own talking is offensive. Some who would be thought criticks, say this humour of his is forced: but to remove that objection, we may consider him first to be naturally of a delicate hearing, as many are, to whom all sharp sounds are unpleasant; and secondly, we may attribute much of it to the peevishness of his age, or the wayward authority of an old man in his own house, where he may make himself obeyed; and to this the poet seems to allude[1] in his name Morose. Besides this, I am assured from divers persons, that Ben Johnson was actually acquainted with such a man, one altogether as ridiculous as he is here represented. Others say, it is not enough to find one man of such an humour; it must be common to more, and the more common the more natural. To prove this, they instance[n] in the best of comical characters, Falstaff. There are many men resembling him; old, fat, merry, cowardly, drunken, amorous, vain, and lying. But to convince these people, I need but tell them, that humour is the ridiculous extravagance of conversation, wherein one man differs from all others. If then it be common, or communicated to many, how differs it from other men's? or what indeed causes it to be ridiculous so much as the singularity of it? As for Falstaff, he is not properly one humour, but a miscellany of humours or images, drawn from so many several men: that wherein he is singular is his wit[2], or those things he says *præter expectatum*, unexpected by the audience; his quick evasions, when you imagine him surprised, which, as they are extremely diverting of themselves, so receive a great addition from his person; for the very sight of such an unwieldy old debauched fellow is a comedy alone. And here, having a place so proper for it, I cannot but enlarge somewhat upon this subject of humour into which I am fallen. The ancients had little of it in

[1] this...seems to allude to, A. [2] in his wit, A.

their comedies; for the τὸ γελοῖον[n] of the old comedy, of which Aristophanes was chief, was not so much to imitate a man, as to make the people laugh at some odd conceit, which had commonly somewhat of unnatural or obscene in it. Thus, when you see Socrates brought upon the stage, you are not to imagine him made ridiculous by the imitation of his actions, but rather by making him perform something very unlike himself; something so childish and absurd, as by comparing it with the gravity of the true Socrates, makes a ridiculous object for the spectators. In their new comedy which succeeded, the poets sought indeed to express the ἦθος, as in their tragedies the πάθος of mankind[n]. But this ἦθος contained only the general characters of men and manners; as old men, lovers, servingmen, courtezans, parasites, and such other persons as we see in their comedies; all which they made alike: that is, one old man or father, one lover, one courtezan, so like another, as if the first of them had begot the rest of every sort: *Ex homine hunc natum dicas*[n]. The same custom they observed likewise in their tragedies. As for the French, though they have the word *humeur* among them, yet they have small use of it in their comedies or farces; they being but ill imitations of the *ridiculum*, or that which stirred up laughter in the old comedy. But among the English 'tis otherwise: where by humour is meant some extravagant habit, passion, or affection, particular (as I said before) to some one person, by the oddness of which, he is immediately distinguished from the rest of men; which being lively and naturally represented, most frequently begets that malicious pleasure in the audience which is testified by laughter; as all things which are deviations from customs[1] are ever the aptest to produce it: though by the way this laughter is only accidental, as the person represented is fantastick or bizarre; but pleasure is essential to it, as the imitation of what is natural. The description of these humours, drawn from the knowledge and observation of particular persons, was the peculiar genius and talent of Ben Johnson; to whose play I now return.

[1] common customes, A.

'Besides Morose, there are at least nine or ten different characters and humours in *The Silent Woman*; all which persons have several concernments of their own, yet are all used by the poet, to the conducting of the main design to perfection. I shall not waste time in commending the writing of this play; but I will give you my opinion, that there is more wit and acuteness of fancy in it than in any of Ben Johnson's. Besides that he has here described the conversation of gentlemen in the persons of True-Wit, and his friends, with more gaiety, air, and freedom, than in the rest of his comedies. For the contrivance of the plot, 'tis extreme[1] elaborate, and yet withal easy, for the λύσις [2], or untying of it, 'tis so admirable, that when it is done, no one of the audience would think the poet could have missed it; and yet it was concealed so much before the last scene, that any other way would sooner have entered into your thoughts. But I dare not take upon me to commend the fabrick of it, because it is altogether so full of art, that I must unravel every scene in it to commend it as I ought. And this excellent contrivance is still the more to be admired, because 'tis comedy, where the persons are only of common rank, and their business private, not elevated by passions or high concernments, as in serious plays. Here every one is a proper judge of all he sees, nothing is represented but that with which he daily converses: so that by consequence all faults lie open to discovery, and few are pardonable. 'Tis this which Horace has judiciously observed:

> *Creditur, ex medio quia res arcessit, habere*
> *Sudoris minimum; sed habet Comedia tanto*
> *Plus oneris, quanto veniæ minus.*[n]

But our poet who was not ignorant of these difficulties, has made use[3] of all advantages; as he who designs a large leap takes his rise from the highest ground. One of these advantages is that which Corneille[n] has laid down as the greatest which can arrive

[1] So C; extream, A and B.

[2] δέσις, A.

[3] had prevailed himself, A.

to any poem, and which he himself could never compass above thrice in all his plays; viz. the making choice of some signal and long-expected day, whereon the action of the play is to depend. This day was that designed by Dauphine for the settling of his uncle's estate upon him; which to compass, he contrives to marry him. That the marriage had been plotted by him long beforehand, is made evident by what he tells True-wit in the second act, that in one moment he had destroyed what he had been raising many months.

'There is another artifice of the poet, which I cannot here omit, because by the frequent practice of it in his comedies he has left it to us almost as a rule; that is, when he has any character or humour wherein he would shew a *coup de Maistre*, or his highest skill, he recommends it to your observation by a pleasant description of it before the person first appears. Thus, in *Bartholomew-Fair* [n] he gives you the pictures of Numps and Cokes, and in this those of Daw, Lafoole, Morose, and the Collegiate Ladies; all which you hear described before you see them. So that before they come upon the stage, you have a longing expectation of them, which prepares you to receive them favourably; and when they are there, even from their first appearance you are so far acquainted with them, that nothing of their humour is lost to you.

'I will observe yet one thing further of this admirable plot; the business of it rises in every act. The second is greater than the first; the third than the second; and so forward to the fifth. There too you see, till the very last scene, new difficulties arising to obstruct the action of the play; and when the audience is brought into despair that the business can naturally be effected, then, and not before, the discovery is made. But that the poet might entertain you with more variety all this while, he reserves some new characters to shew you, which he opens not till the second and third act; in the second Morose, Daw, the Barber, and Otter; in the third the Collegiate Ladies: all which he moves afterwards in by-walks, or under-plots, as diversions to the main design, lest it should grow tedious, though they are still naturally joined with it, and somewhere or other subservient to it. Thus, like a skilful chess-player[1], by little and little he draws out his men, and makes his pawns of use to his greater persons.

'If this comedy[n] and some others of his, were translated into French prose, (which would now be no wonder to them, since Moliere has lately given them plays out of verse, which have not displeased them,) I believe the controversy would soon be decided betwixt the two nations, even making them the judges. But we need not call our heroes[2] to our aid. Be it spoken to the honour of the English, our nation can never want in any age such who are able to dispute the empire of wit with any people in the universe. And though the fury of a civil war, and power for twenty years together abandoned to a barbarous race of men, enemies of all good learning, had buried the muses under the ruins of monarchy; yet, with the restoration of our happiness, we see revived poesy lifting up its head, and already shaking off the rubbish which lay so heavy on it. We have seen since his majesty's return, many dramatick poems which yield not to those of any foreign nation, and which deserve all laurels but the English. I will set aside flattery and envy: it cannot be denied but we have had some little blemish either in the plot or writing of all those plays which have been made within these seven years; (and perhaps there is no nation in the world so quick to discern them, or so difficult to pardon them, as ours:) yet if we can persuade ourselves to use the candour of that poet, who, though the most severe of criticks, has left us this caution by which to moderate our censures—

> *——ubi plura nitent in carmine, non ego paucis*
> *offendar maculis;—*[n]

if, in consideration of their many and great beauties, we can wink at some slight and little imperfections, if we, I say, can be thus

[1] so C; Chest-player, A and B.
[2] so C; Hero's, A and B.

equal to ourselves, I ask no favour from the French. And if I do not venture upon any particular judgment of our late plays, 'tis out of the consideration which an ancient writer gives me: *vivorum, ut magna admiratio, ita censura difficilis*[n]: betwixt the extremes of admiration and malice, 'tis hard to judge uprightly of the living. Only I think it may be permitted me to say, that as it is no lessening to us to yield to some plays, and those not many, of our own nation in the last age, so can it be no addition to pronounce of our present poets, that they have far surpassed all the ancients, and the modern writers of other countries[1].'

This was[2] the substance of what was then spoke on that occasion; and Lisideius, I think, was going to reply, when he was prevented thus by Crites: 'I am confident,' said he, 'that the most material things that can be said have been already urged on either side; if they have not, I must beg of Lisideius that he will defer his answer till another time: for I confess I have a joint quarrel to you both, because you have concluded, without any reason given for it, that rhyme is proper for the stage. I will not dispute how ancient it hath been among us to write this way; perhaps our ancestors knew no better till Shakespeare's time. I will grant it was not altogether left by him, and that Fletcher and Ben Johnson used it frequently in their Pastorals, and sometimes in other plays. Farther,—I will not argue whether we received it originally from our own countrymen, or from the French; for that is an inquiry of as little benefit, as theirs who, in the midst of the late plague[3], were not so solicitous to provide against it, as to know whether we had it from the malignity of our own air, or by transportation from Holland. I have therefore only to affirm, that it is not allowable in serious plays; for comedies, I find you already concluding with me. To prove this, I might satisfy myself to tell you, how much in vain it is for you to strive against the stream of the people's inclination; the greatest part of which are

[1] so C; Countreys, A and B.

[2] This, my Lord, was, A.

[3] the great plague, A.

prepossessed so much with those excellent plays of Shakespeare, Fletcher, and Ben Johnson, which have been written out of rhyme, that except you could bring them such as were written better in it, and those too by persons of equal reputation with them, it will be impossible for you to gain your cause with them, who will still be judges. This it is to which, in fine, all your reasons must submit. The unanimous consent of an audience is so powerful, that even Julius Cæsar, (as Macrobius reports of him,) when he was perpetual dictator, was not able to balance it on the other side; but when Laberious, a Roman Knight, at his request contended in the *Mime* with another poet[n], he was forced to cry out, *Etiam favente me victus es, Laberi*[1]. But I will not on his occasion take the advantage of the greater number, but only urge such reasons against rhyme, as I find in the writings of those who have argued for the other way. First then, I am of opinion, that rhyme is unnatural in a play, because dialogue there is presented as the effect of sudden thought: for a play is the imitation of nature; and since no man, without premeditation speaks in rhyme, neither ought he to do it on the stage. This hinders not but the fancy may be there elevated to an higher pitch of thought than it is in ordinary discourse; for there is a probability that men of excellent and quick parts may speak noble things *extempore*: but those thoughts are never fettered with the numbers or sound of verse without study, and therefore it cannot be but unnatural to present the most free way of speaking in that which is the most constrained. For this reason, says Aristotle[n], 'tis best to write tragedy in that kind of verse which is the least such, or which is nearest prose: and this amongst the ancients was the Iambick, and with us is blank verse, or the measure of verse kept exactly without rhyme. These numbers therefore are fittest for a play; the others for a paper of verses, or a poem; blank verse being as much below them, as rhyme is improper for the drama. And if it be objected that neither are blank verses

[1] Liberi, A.

made *extempore*, yet, as nearest nature, they are still to be preferred.—But there are two particular exceptions, which many besides myself have had to verse; by which it will appear yet more plainly how improper it is in plays. And the first of them is grounded on that very reason for which some have commended rhyme; they say, the quickness of repartees in argumentative scenes receives an ornament from verse. Now what is more unreasonable than to imagine that a man should not only light upon the wit[1], but the rhyme too, upon the sudden? This nicking[n] of him who spoke before both in sound and measure, is so great an happiness, that you must at least suppose the persons of your play to be born poets: *Arcades omnes, et cantare pares, et respondereparati*[n]: they must have arrived to the degree of *quicquid conabar dicere*[n];—to make verses almost whether they will or no. If they are anything below this, it will look rather like the design of two, than the answer of one: it will appear that your actors hold intelligence together; that they perform their tricks like fortune-tellers, by confederacy. The hand of art will be too visible in it, against that maxim of all professions—*Ars est celare artem*; that it is the greatest perfection of art to keep itself undiscovered. Nor will it serve you to object, that however you manage it, 'tis still known to be a play; and, consequently, the dialogue of two persons understood to be the labour of one poet. For a play is still an imitation of nature; we know we are to be deceived, and we desire to be so; but no man ever was deceived but with a probability of truth; for who will suffer a gross lie to be fastened on him? Thus we sufficiently understand, that the scenes which represent cities and countries to us are not really such, but only painted on boards and canvas; but shall that excuse the ill painture[n] or designment[n] of them? Nay, rather ought they not to be laboured with so much the more diligence and exactness, to help the imagination? since the mind of man does naturally tend to[2] truth; and therefore the nearer anything comes to the imitation of it, the more it pleases.

[1] so A; not only imagine the Wit, B.

[2] tend to and seek after, A

'Thus, you see, your rhyme is uncapable of expressing the greatest thoughts naturally, and the lowest it cannot with any grace: for what is more unbefitting the majesty of verse, than to call a servant, or bid a door be shut in rhyme? and yet you are often forced on this miserable necessity[1]. But verse, you say, circumscribes a quick and luxuriant fancy, which would extend itself too far on every subject, did not the labour which is required to well-turned and polished rhyme, set bounds to it. Yet this argument, if granted, would only prove that we may write better in verse, but not more naturally. Neither is it able to evince that; for he who wants judgment to confine his fancy in blank verse, may want it as much in rhyme: and he who has it will avoid errors in both kinds. Latin verse was as great a confinement to the imagination of those poets, as rhyme to ours; and yet you find Ovid saying too much on every subject. *Nescivit* (says Seneca) *quod bene cessit relinquere*[n]: of which he gives you one famous instance in his description of the deluge:

> *Omnia pontus erat, deerant quoque litora ponto*[n].
> Now all was sea, not had that sea a shore.

Thus Ovid's fancy was not limited by verse, and Virgil needed not verse to have bounded his.

'In our own language we see Ben Johnson confining himself to what ought to be said, even in the liberty of blank verse; and yet Corneille, the most judicious of the French poets, is still varying the same sense an hundreds ways, and dwelling eternally on the same subject, though confined by rhyme. Some other exceptions I have to verse; but since these[2] I have named are for the most part already publick, I conceive it reasonable they should first be answered.'

'It concerns me less than any,' said Neander, (seeing he had ended,) 'to reply to this discourse; because when I should have proved that verse may be natural in plays, yet I should always be

[1] this mis. nec. you are forc'd upon, A.

[2] but being these, A.

ready to confess, that those which I have written in this kind[n] come short of that perfection which is required. Yet since you are pleased I should undertake this province, I will do it, though with all imaginable respect and deference, both to that person[n] from whom you have borrowed your strongest arguments, and to whose judgement, when I have said all, I finally submit. But before I proceed to answer your objections, I must first remember you, that I exclude all comedy from my defence; and next that I deny not but blank verse may be also used; and content myself only to assert, that in serious plays where the subject and characters are great, and the plot unmixed with mirth, which might allay or divert these concernments which are produced, rhyme is there as natural and more effectual than blank verse.

'And now having laid down this as a foundation,—to begin with Crites,—I must crave leave to tell him, that some of his arguments against rhyme reach no farther than, from the faults or defects of ill rhyme, to conclude against the use of it in general. May not I conclude against blank verse by the same reason? If the words of some poets who writes in it, are either ill chosen, or ill placed, which makes not only rhyme, but all kind of verse in any language unnatural, shall I, for their vicious affectation, condemn those excellent lines of Fletcher, which are written in that kind? Is there any thing in rhyme more constrained than this line in blank verse?—*I heaven invoke, and strong resistance make*; where you see both the clauses are placed unnaturally, that is, contrary to the common way of speaking, and that without the excuse of a rhyme to cause it: yet you would think me very ridiculous, if I should accuse the stubbornness of blank verse for this, and not rather the stiffness of the poet. Therefore, Crites, you must either prove that words, though well chosen, and duly placed, yet render not rhyme natural in itself; or that, however natural and easy the rhyme may be, yet it is not proper for a play. If you insist on the former part, I would ask you, what other conditions are required to make rhyme natural in itself, besides an election of apt words, and a right dispositon[1] of them? For the due choice of your words expresses your sense naturally, and the due placing them adapts the rhyme to it. If you object that one verse may be made for the sake of another, though both the words and rhyme be apt, I answer, it cannot possibly so fall out; for either there is a dependence of sense betwixt the first line and the second, or there is none: if there be that connection, then in the natural position of the words the latter line must of necessity flow from the former; if there be no dependance, yet still the due ordering of words makes the last line as natural in itself as the other: so that the necessity of a rhyme never forces any but bad or lazy writers to say what they would not otherwise. 'Tis true, there is both care and art required to write in verse. A good poet never establishes[2] the first line, till he has sought out such a rhyme as may fit the sense, already prepared to heighten the second: many times the close of the sense falls into the middle of the next verse, or farther off, and he may often prevail himself[h] of the same advantages in English which Virgil had in Latin,—he may break off in the hemystich, and begin another line. Indeed, the not observing these two last things, makes plays which are writ in verse, so tedious: for though, most commonly, the sense is to be confined to the couplet, yet nothing that does *pepetuo tenore fluere*, run in the same channel, can please always. 'Tis like the murmuring of a stream, which not varying in the fall, causes at first attention, at last drowsiness. Variety of cadences is the best rule; the greatest help to the actors, and refreshment to the audience.

'If then verse may be made natural in itself, how becomes it unnatural in[3] a play? You say the stage is the representation of nature, and no man in ordinary conversation speaks in rhyme. But you foresaw when you said this, that it might be answered—neither does any man speak in blank verse, or in measure without rhyme. Therefore you concluded, that which is nearest nature is

[1] diposing, A. [2] concludes upon, A.

[3] improper to, A.

still to be preferred. But you took no notice that rhyme might be made as natural as blank verse, by the well placing of the words, &c. All the differences between them, when they are both correct, is, the sound in one, which the other wants; and if so, the sweetness of it, and all the advantage resulting from it, which are handled in the Preface to *The Rival Ladies*, will yet stand good. As for that place of Aristotle, where he says, plays should be writ in that kind of verse which is nearest prose, it makes little for you; blank verse being properly but measured prose. Now measure alone, in any modern language, does not constitute verse; those of the ancients in Greek and Latin consisted in quality of words, and a determinate number of feet. But when, by the inundation of the Goths and Vandals into Italy, new languages were introduced[1], and barbarously mingles with the Latin, of which the Italian, Spanish, French, and ours, (made out of them and the Teutonick,) are dialects, a new way of poesy was practised; new, I say, in those countries, for in all probability it was that of the conquerors in their own nations: at least we are able to prove, that the eastern people have used it from all antiquity[2 n]. This new way consisted in measure or number of feet, and rhyme; the sweetness of rhyme, and observation of accent, supplying the place of quantity in words, which could neither exactly be observed by those barbarians, who knew not the rules of it, neither was it suitable to their tongues, as it had been to the Greek and Latin. No man is tied in modern poesy to observe any farther rule in the feet of his verse, but that they be dissyllables; whether Spondee, Trochee, or Iambick, it matters not; only he is obliged to rhyme: neither do the Spanish, French, Italian, or Germans, acknowledge at all, or very rarely, any such kind of poesy as blank verse amongst them. Therefore, at most 'tis but a poetick prose, a *sermo pedestris*; and as such, most fit for comedies, where I acknowledge rhyme to be improper.— Farther; as to that quotation of Aristotle, our couplet verses may

[1] brought in, A.

[2] A *om.* at least...antiquity, and the note.

be rendered as near prose as blank verse itself, by using those advantages I lately named,—as breaks in an hemistich, or running the sense into another line,—thereby making art and and order appear as loose and free as nature: or not tying ourselves to couplets strictly, we may use the benefit of the Pindarick way practised in *The Siege of Rhodes*[n]; where the numbers vary, and the rhyme is disposed carelessly, and far from often chyming. Neither is that other advantage of the ancients to be despised, of changing the kind of verse when they please, with the change of the scene, or some new entrance; for they confine not themselves always to iambicks, but extend their liberty to all lyrick numbers, and sometimes even to hexameter[n]. But I need not go so far to prove that rhyme, as it succeeds to all other offices of Greek and Latin verse, so especially to this of plays, since the custom of nations[1] at this day confirms it; the French[2], Italian,[n] and Spanish tragedies are generally writ in it; and sure the universal consent of the most civilized parts of the world, ought in this, as it doth in other customs, to[3] include the rest.

'But perhaps you may tell me, I have proposed such a way to make rhyme natural, and consequently proper to plays, as is unpracticable; and that I shall scarce find six or eight lines together in any play, where the words are so placed and chosen as is required to make it natural. I answer, no poet need constrain himself at all times to it. It is enough he makes it his general rule; for I deny not but sometimes there may be a greatness in placing the words otherwise; and sometimes they may sound better; sometimes also the variety itself is excuse enough. But if, for the most part, the words be placed as they are in the negligence of prose, it is sufficient to denominate the way practicable; for we esteem that to be such, which in the trial oftner succeeds than misses. And thus far you may find the practice made good in many plays: where you do not, remember still, that if you cannot find six natural rhymes together, it will be as hard for you to produce as many lines in blank verse, even

[1] all Nations, A. [2] all the French, &c,. A. [3] A *om.* to.

among the greatest of our poets, against which I cannot make some reasonable exception.

'And this, Sir, calls to my remembrance the beginning of your discourse, where you told us we should never find the audience favourable to this kind of writing, till we could produce as good plays in rhyme, as Ben Johnson, Fletcher, and Shakespeare, has writ out of it. But it is to raise envy to the living, to compare them with the dead. They are honoured, and almost adored by us, as they deserve; neither do I know any so presumptuous of themselves as to contend with them. Yet give me leave to say thus much, without injury to their ashes; that not only we shall never equal them, but they could never equal themselves, were they to rise and write again. We acknowledge them our fathers in wit; but they have ruined their estates themselves, before they came to their children's hands. There is scarce an humour, a character, or any kind of plot, which they have not used[1]. All comes sullied or wasted to us: and were they to entertain this age, they could not now[2] make so plenteous treatments out of such decayed fortunes. This therefore will be a good argument to us, either not to write at all, or to attempt some other way. There is no bays to be expected in their walks: *tentanda via est, qua me quoque possum tollere humo*[n].

This way of writing in verse they have only left free to us; our age is arrived to a perfection in it, which they never knew; and which (if we may guess by what of theirs we have seen in verse, as *The Faithful Shepherdess*, and *Sad Shepherd*) 'tis probable they never could have reached. For the genius of every age is different; and though ours excel in this, I deny not but to imitate nature in that perfection which they did in prose, is a greater commendation than to write in verse exactly. As for what you have added—that the people are not generally inclined to like this way,—if it were true, it would be no wonder, that betwixt the shaking off an old habit, and the introducing of a new, there

[1] blown upon, A. [2] A *om.*

should be difficulty. Do we not see them stick to Hopkins' and Sternhold's psalms, and forsake those of David, I mean Sandys his translation[n] of them? If by the people you understand the multitude, the οἱ πολλοί, 'tis no matter what they think; they are sometimes in the right, sometimes in the wrong: their judgment is a mere lottery. *Est ubi plebs rectè putat, est ubi peccat*[n]. Horace says it of the vulgar, judging poesy. But if you mean the mixed audience of the populace and the noblesse, I dare confidently affirm that a great part of the latter sort are already favourable to verse; and that no serious plays written since the king's return have been more kindly received by them, than *The Siege of Rhodes, the Mustapha*[n], *The Indian Queen, and Indian Emperor*.

'But I come now to the inference of your first argument. You said that[1] the dialogue of plays is presented as the effect of sudden thought, but no man speaks suddenly, or *extempore*, in rhyme; and you inferred from thence, that rhyme, which you acknowledge to be proper to epick poesy, cannot equally be proper to dramatick, unless we could suppose all men born so much more than poets, that verses should be made in them, not by them.

'It has been formerly urged by you, and confessed by me, that since no man spoke any kind of verse *extempore*, that which was nearest nature was to be preferred. I answer you, therefore, by distinguishing betwixt what is nearest to the nature of comedy, which is the imitation of common persons and ordinary speaking, and what is nearest the nature of a serious play: this last is indeed the representation of nature, but 'tis nature wrought up to an highter pitch. The plot, the characters, the wit, the passions, the descriptions, are all exalted above the level of common converse, as high as the imagination of the poet can carry them, with proportion to verisimility. Tragedy, we know, is wont to image to us the minds and fortunes of noble persons, and to portray these

[1] A *om*.

exactly; heroick rhyme is nearest nature, as being the noblest kind of modern verse.

Indignatur enim privatis et prope socco
Dignis carminibus narrari cœna Thyestæ[n]—

says Horace: and in another place,

Effutire leves indigna tragœdia versus[n]—.

Blank verse is acknowledged to be too low for a poem, nay more, for a paper of verses; but if too low for an ordinary sonnet[n], how much more for tragedy, which is by Aristotle, in the dispute betwixt the epick poesy and the dramatick, for many reasons he there alledges, ranked above it?[n]

'But setting this defence aside, your argument is almost as strong against the use of rhyme in poems as in plays; for the epick way is every where interlaced with dialogue, or discoursive scenes; and therefore you must either grant rhyme to be improper there, which is contrary to your assertion, or admit it into plays by the same title which you have given it to poems. For though tragedy by justly preferred above the other, yet there is a great affinity between them, as may easily be discovered in that definition of a play which Lisideius gave us. The *genus* of them is the same,—a just and lively image of human nature, in its actions, passions, and traverses of fortune: so is the end,—namely, for the delight and benefit of mankind. The characters and persons and still the same, viz. the greatest of both sorts; only the manner of acquainting us with those actions, passions, and fortunes, is different. Tragedy performs it *viva voce*, or by action, in dialogue; wherein it excels the epick poem, which does it chiefly by narration, and therefore is not so lively an image of human nature. However, the agreement betwixt them is such, that if rhyme be proper for one, it must be for the other. Verse, 'tis, true, is not the effect of sudden thought; but this hinders not that sudden thought may be represented in verse, since those thoughts are such as must be higher than nature can raise them without premeditation, especially to a continuance of them, even out of verse; and consequently you cannot imagine them to have been sudden either in the poet or in the actors. A play, as I have said, to be like nature, is to be set above it; as statues which are placed on high are made greater than the life, that they may descend to the sight in their just proportion.

'Perhaps I have insisted too long on this objection; but the clearing of it will make my stay shorter on the rest. You tell us, Crites, that rhyme appears most unnatural in repartees, or short replies: when he who answers, (it being presumed he knew not what the other would say, yet) makes up that part of the verse which was left incomplete, and supplies both the sound and measure of it. This, you say, looks rather like the confederacy of two, than the answer of one.

'This, I confess, is an objection which is in every man's[1] mouth, who loves not rhyme: but suppose, I beseech you, the repartee were made only in blank verse, might not part of the same argument be turned against you? for the measure is as often supplied there, as it is in rhyme; the latter half of the hemistich as commonly made up, or a second line subjoined as a reply to the former; which any one leaf in Johnson's plays will sufficiently clear to you. You will often find in the Greek tragedians, and in Seneca, that when a scene grows up into the warmth of repartees, which is the close fighting of it, the latter part of the trimeter is supplied by him who answers; and yet it was never observed as a fault in them by any of the ancient or modern criticks. The case is the same in our verse, as it was in theirs; rhyme to us being in lieu of quantity to them. But if no latitude is to be allowed a poet, you take from him not only his licence of *quidlibet audendi*[n], but you tie him up in a straiter compass than you would a philosopher. This is indeed *Musas colere severiores*[n]. You would have him follow nature, but he must follow her on foot: you have dismounted him from his Pegasus.

[1] ones, A.

But you tell us, this supplying the last half of a verse, or adjoining a whole second to the former, looks more like the design of two, than the answer of one. Suppose we acknowledge it: how comes this confederacy to be more displeasing to you, than in a dance which is well contrived? You see there the united design of many persons to make up one figure: after they have separated themselves in many petty divisions, they rejoin one by one into a gross: the confederacy is plain amongst them, for chance could never produce anything so beautiful; and yet there is nothing in it, that shocks your sight. I acknowledge the hand of art appears in repartee, as of necessity it must in all kind of verse. But there is also the quick and poynant brevity of it (which is an high imitation of nature in those sudden gusts of passion) to mingle with it; and this, joined with the cadency and sweetness of the rhyme, leaves nothing in the soul of the hearer to desire. 'Tis an art which appears; but it appears only like the shadowings of painture, which being to cause the rounding of it, cannot be absent; but while that is considered, they are lost: so while we attend to the other beauties of the matter, the care and labour of the rhyme is carried from us, or at least drowned in its own sweetness, as bees are sometimes buried in their honey. When a poet has found the repartee, the last perfection he can add to it, is to put it into verse. However good the thought may be, however apt the words in which 'tis couched, yet he finds himself at a little unrest, whilc rhyme is wanting: he cannot leave it till that comes naturally, and then is at ease, and sits down contented.

'From replies, which are the most elevated thoughts of verse, you pass to those which are most mean, and which[1] are common with the lowest of houshold conversation. In these, you say, the majesty of verse suffers. You instance in the calling of a servant, or commanding a door to be shut, in rhyme. This, Crites, is a good observation of your's, but no argument: for it proves no more but that such thoughts should be waved, as often as may

[1] to the most mean ones, those which, A.

be, by the address of the poet. But suppose they are necessary in the places where he uses them, yet there is no need to put them into rhyme. He may place them in the beginning of a verse, and break it off, as unfit, when so debased, for any other use; or granting the worst,—that they require more room than the hemistich will allow, yet still there is a choice to be made of the best words, and least vulgar, (provided they be apt,) to express such thoughts. Many have blamed rhyme in general, for this fault, when the poet with a little care might have redressed it. But they do it with no more justice, than if English poesy should be made ridiculous for the sake of the Water-poet's[n] rhymes. Our language is noble, full, and significant; and I know not why he who is master of it may not clothe ordinary things in it as decently as the Latin, if he use the same diligence in his choice of words: *delectus verborum origo est eloquentioe*[n]. It was the saying of Julius Cæsar, one so curious in his, that none of them can be changed but for a worse. One would think, *unlock the door*, was a thing as vulgar as could be spoken; and yet Seneca could make it sound high and lofty in his Latin:

Reserate clusos regii postes laris[n].
Set wide the palace gates.

'But I turn from his exception, both because it happens not above twice or thrice in any play that those vulgar thoughts are used; and then too, (were there no other apology to be made, yet,) the necessity of them, which is alike in all kind of writing, may excuse them. For if they are little and mean in rhyme, they are of consequence such in blank verse[1]. Besides that the great eagerness and precipitation with which they are spoken, makes us rather mind the substance than the dress; that for which they are spoken, rather than what is spoke. For they are always the effect of some hasty concernment, and something of consequence depends on them.

[1] A *om.* For it they...blank verse.

'Thus, Crites, I have endeavoured to answer your objections; it remains only that I should vindicate an argument for verse, which you have gone about to overthrow. It had formerly been said[n], that the easiness of blank verse renders the poet too luxuriant, but that the labour of rhyme bounds and circumscribes an over-fruitful fancy; the sense[1] there being commonly confined to the couplet, and the words so ordered that the rhyme naturally follows them, not they the rhyme. To this you answered, that it was no argument to the question in hand; for the dispute was not which way a man may write best, but which is most proper for the subject on which he writes.

'First, give me leave, Sir, to remember you, that the argument against which you raised this objection, was only secondary: it was built on this hypothesis,—that to write in verse was proper for serious plays. Which supposition being granted, (as it was briefly made out in that discourse, by shewing how verse might be made natural,) it asserted, that this way of writing was an help to the poet's judgment, by puting bounds to a wild overflowing fancy. I think, therefore, it will not be hard for me to make good what it was to prove on that supposition[2]. But you add, that were this let pass, yet he who wants judgment in the liberty of his fancy, may as well shew the defect of it when he is confined to verse; for he who has judgment will avoid errors, and he who has it not, will commit them in all kinds of writing.

This argument, as you have taken it from a most acute person[n], so I confess it carries much weight in it: but by using the word judgment here indefinitely, you seem to have put a fallacy upon us. I grant, he who has judgment, that is, so profound, so strong, or rather[3] so infallible a judgment, that he needs no helps to keep it always poised and upright, will commit no faults either in rhyme or out of it. And on the other extreme, he who has a judgment so weak and crazed that no helps can correct or amend it, shall

[1] so A; scene, B and C.

[2] A *om.* on that supposition

[3] A *om.* or rather

write scurvily out of rhyme, and worse in it. But the first of these judgments is nowhere to be found, and the latter is not fit to write at all. To speak therefore of judgment as it is in the best poets; they who have the greatest proportion of it, want other helps than from it, within. As for example, you would be loth to say, that he who is[1] endowed with a sound judgment has[2] no need of history, geography, or moral philosophy, to write correctly. Judgment is indeed the master-workman in a play; but he requires many subordinate hands, many tools to his assistance. And verse I affirm to be one of these; 'tis a rule and line by which he keeps his building compact and even, which otherwise lawless imagination would raise either irregularly or loosely; at least, if the poet commits errors with this help, he would make greater and more without it:—'tis, in short, a slow and painful, but the surest kind of working. Ovid, whom you accuse for luxuriancy in verse, had perhaps been farther guilty of it, had he writ in prose. And for your instance of Ben Johnson, who, you say, writ exactly without the help of rhyme; you are to remember, 'tis only an aid to a luxuriant fancy, which his was not: as he did not want imagination, so none ever said he had much to spare. Neither was verse then refined so much, to be an help to that age, as it is to ours. Thus then the second thoughts being usually the best, as receiving the maturest digestion from judgment, and the last and most mature product of those thoughts being artful and laboured verse, it may well be inferred, that verse is a great help to a luxuriant fancy; and this is what that argument which you opposed was to evince.'

Neander was pursuing this discourse so eagerly, that Eugenius had called to him twice or thrice, ere he took notice that the barge stood still, and that they were at the foot of Somerset-stairs, where they had appointed it to land. The company were all sorry to separate so soon, though a great part of the evening

[1] was, A. [2] had, A.

was already spent; and stood a-while looking back on the water, upon which the moon-beams played[1], and made it appear like floating quicksilver: at last they went up though a crowd of French people, who were merrily dancing in the open air, and nothing concerned for the noise of guns which had alarmed the town that afternoon. Walking thence together to the Piazze[n], they parted there; Eugenius and Lisideius to some pleasant appointment they had made, and Crites and Neander to their several lodgings.

[1] which the moon beams played upon, A.

A Defence[1]

OF AN ESSAY

OF DRAMATIC POESY[*]

THE former edition of *The Indian Emperor* being full of faults, which had escaped the printer, I have been willing to overlook this second with more care; and though I could not allow myself so much time as was necessary, yet, by that little I have done, the press is freed from some gross errors which it had to answer

---

[1] The text of the 'Defence' is reprinted from the original edition of 1668 (the only one published in Dryden's life-time), a copy of which is in the British Museum; it is prefixed as a sort of Introduction to the *second* edition of Dryden's *Indian Emperor*.

[*] Our author married, probably about the year 1664, Lady Elizabeth Howard, sister of Sir Robert Howard knt., and daughter of Thomas, the first Earl of Berkshire [ancestor of the present Earl of Suffolk]. In 1660 he had addressed some complimentary verses to Sir Robert, which were prefixed to his poems, published in 8vo. in that year. In 1666 they appear to have been on good terms; Dryden having then addressed to him an encomiastick Epistle in prose, which is dated from Charleton, in Wiltshire (the seat of the Earl of Berkshire), and was prefixed to his Annus *Mirabilis*, published in 8vo. in 1667, by Sir Robert Howard, who revised the sheets at the press for the author, who was then in the country; and in the Epistle he describes him as one whom he knew

for before. As for the more material faults of writing, which are properly mine, though I see many of them, I want leisure to amend them. 'Tis enough for those who make one poem the business of their lives, to leave that correct: yet, excepting Virgil, I never met with any which was so in any language.

But while I was thus employed about this impression, there came to my hands a new printed play, called, *The Great Favourite*, or *The Duke of Lerma*; the author of which, a noble and most ingenious person, has done me the favour to make some observations and animadversions upon my *Dramatique Essay*. I must confess he might have better consulted his reputation, than by matching himself with so weak an adversary. But if his honour be diminished in the choice of his antagonist, it is sufficiently recompensed in the election of his cause: which being the weaker, in all appearance, as combating the received opinions of the best ancient and modern authors, will add to his glory, if he overcome, and to the opinion of his generosity, if he be vanquished: since he ingages at so great odds, and, so like a cavalier, undertakes the protection of the weaker party. I have only to fear on my own behalf, that so good a cause as mine may

---

not to be of the number of those, *qui carpere amicos suos judicium vocant*. In *the Essay on Dramatick Poesy*, as we have already seen, he speaks of Sir Robert Howard with great respect. That gentleman, however, having in 1668 published [in the preface to his tragedy, *The Duke of Lerma*] reflections on the Essay, our author retorted in the following observations, which are found prefixed to the second edition of *The Indian Emperor*, published in the same year. In many copies, however, of that edition, they are wanting; nor were they reprinted in any other edition of that play which appeared in the life-time of the author: so that it should seem he was induced by good nature, or the interposition of friends, to suppress this witty and severe replication. One of the lampoons of the time gives a more invidious turn to this suppression, and insinuates that he was compelled to retract. They lived afterwards probably in good correspondence together; at least, it appears from an original letter of our author now before me, that towards the close of his life they were on friendly terms. (Malone.)

not suffer by my ill management, or weak defence; yet I cannot in honour but take the glove, when 'tis offered me: though I am only a champion by succession; and no more able to defend the right of Aristotle and Horace, than an infant Dimock[n] to maintain the title of a King.

For my own concernment in the controvesie, it is so small, that I can easily be contended to be driven from a new notions of Dramatique Poesie; especially by one, who has the reputation of understanding all things: and I might justly make that excuse for my yielding to him, which the Philosopher[n] made to the Emperor, —*why should I offer to contend with him, who is master of more than twenty legions of arts and sciences*? But I am forced to fight, and therefore it will be no shame to be overcome.

Yet I am so much his servant, as not to meddle with any thing which does not concern me in his Preface; therefore, I leave the good sense and other excellencies of the first twenty lines to be considered by the critiques. As for the play of *The Duke of Lerma*, having so much altered and beautified it, as he has done, it can justly belong to none but him. Indeed, they must be extream ignorant as well as envious, who would rob him of that honour; for you see him putting in his claim to it, even in the first two lines:

Repulse upon repulse, like waves thrown back,
That slide to hang upon obdurate rocks.

After this, let detraction do its worst; for if this be not his, it deserves to be. For my part, I declare for distributive justice; and from this and what follows, he certainly deserves *those advantages which he acknowledges to have received from the opinion of sober men.*

In the next place, I must beg leave to observe his great address in courting the reader to his party. For intending to assault all poets, both ancient and modern, he discovers not his whole design at once, but seems only to aim at me, and attacques me on my weakest side, my defence of verse.

To begin with me,—he gives me the compellation of *The Author of a Dramatique Essay*, which is a little discourse in dialogue, for the most part borrowed from the observations of others: therefore, that I may not be wanting to him in civility, I return his compliment by calling him *The Author of The Duke of Lerma*.

But (that I may pass over his salute) he takes notice of my great pains to prove rhyme as natural in a serious play, and more effectual than blanck verse. Thus, indeed, I did state the question; but he tells me, *I pursue that which I call natural in a wrong application: for 'tis not the question whether rhyme or not rhyme be best or most natural for a serious subject, but what is nearest the nature of that it represents*.

If I have formerly mistaken the question, I must confess my ignorance so far, as to say I continue still in my mistake: but he ought to have proved that I mistook it; for it is yet but *gratis dictum*: I still shall think I have gained my point, if I can prove that rhyme is best or most natural for a serious subject. As for the question as he states it, whether rhyme be nearest the nature of what it represents, I wonder he should think me so ridiculous as to dispute whether prose or verse be nearest to ordinary conversation.

It still remains for him to prove his inference,—that, since verse is granted to be more remote than prose from ordinary conversation, therefore no serious plays ought to be writ in verse: and when he clearly makes that good, I will acknowledge his victory as absolute as he can desire it.

The question now is, which of us two has mistaken it; and if it appear I have not, the world will suspect *what gentleman that was, who was allowed to speak twice in parliament, because he had not yet spoken to the question*; and perhaps conclude it to be the same, who, 'tis reported, maintained a contradiction *in terminis*, in the face of three hundred persons.

But to return to verse; whether it be natural or not in plays, is a problem which is not demonstrable of either side: 'tis enough for me that he acknowledges he had rather read good verse than prose: for if all the enemies of verse will confess as much, I shall not need to prove that it is natural, I am satisfied, if it cause delight: for delight is the chief, if not the only[n], end of poesie: instruction can be admitted but in the second place; for poesie only instructs as it delights. 'Tis true, that to imitate well is a poet's work; but to affect the soul, and excite the passions, and above all to move admiration, which is the delight of serious plays, a bare imitation will not serve. The converse, therefore, which a poet is to imitate, must be heightened with all the arts and ornaments of poesie; and must be such, as, strictly considered, could never be supposed spoken by any without premeditation.

As for what he urges, that *a play will still be supposed to be a composition of several persons speaking extempore; and that good verses are the hardest things which can be imagined to be so spoken*; I must crave leave to dissent from his opinion, as to the former part of it: for, if I am not deceived, a play is supposed to be the work of the poet, imitating or representing the conversation of several persons; and this I think to be as clear, as he thinks the contrary.

But I will be bolder, and do not doubt to make it good, though a paradox, that one great reason why prose is not to be used in serious plays, is, because it is too near the nature of converse: there may be too great a likeness; as the most skilful painters affirm, that there may be too near a resemblance in a picture: to take every lineament and feature, is not to make an excellent piece; but to take so much only as will make a beautiful resemblance of the whole; and, with an ingenious flattery of nature, to heighten the beauties of some parts, and hide the deformities of the rest. For so says Horace:

> *Ut pictura poesis erit . . . . . .*
> *Hœc amat obscurum, vult hœc sub luce videri,*
> *Judicis argutum quœ non formidat acumen*[n].

————————*et quœ*
Desperat tractata nitescere posse, relinquit[n].

In *Bartholomew Fair*, or the lowest kind of comedy, that degree of heightning is used, which is proper to set off that subject. 'Tis true the author was not there to go out of prose, as he does in his higher arguments of comedy, *The Fox*, and *Alchymist*; yet he does so raise his matter in that prose, as to render it delightful; which he could never have performed, had he only said or done those very things that are daily spoken or practised in the Fair; for then the Fair itself would be as full of pleasure to an ingenious person as the play; which was manifestly see it is not. But he hath made an excellent lazar[n] of it: the copy is of price, though the original be vile. You see in *Catiline* and *Sejanus*, where the argument is great, he sometimes ascends to verse, which shews he thought it not unnatural in serious plays: and had his genius been as proper for rhyme, as it was for humour, or had the age in which he lived attained to as much knowledge in verse as ours, it is probable he would have adorned those subjects with that kind of writing.

Thus prose, though the rightful prince, yet is by common consent deposed, as too weak for the government of serious plays; and he failing, there now start up two competitors; one the nearer in blood, which is blanck verse; the other more fit for the ends of government, which is rhyme. Blanck verse is, indeed, the nearer prose, but he is blemished with the weakness of his predecessor. Rhyme (for I will deal clearly) has somewhat of the usurper in him; but he is brave and generous, and his dominion pleasing. For this reason of delight, the Ancients (whom I will still believe as wise as those who so confidently correct them) wrote all their tragedies in verse, though they knew it most remote from conversation.

But I perceive I am falling into the danger of another rebuke from my opponent; for when I plead that the Ancients used verse, I prove not that they would have admitted rhyme, had it then been written: all I can say is only this; that it seems to have succeeded verse by the general consent of poets in all modern languages: for almost all their serious plays are written in it: which, though it be no demonstration that therefore they ought to be so, yet at least the practice first, and then the continuation of it, shews that it attained the end,—which was to please; and if that cannot be compassed here, I will be the first who shall lay it down. For I confess my chief endeavours are to delight the age in which I live. If the humour of this be for low comedy, small accidents, and raillery, I will force my genius to obey it, though with more reputation I could write in verse. I know I am not so fitted by nature to write comedy: I want that gayety of humour which is required to it. My conversation[n] is slow and dull, my humour saturnine and reserved: in short, I am none of those who endeavour to break jests in company, or make reparties. So that those who decry my comedies do me no injury, except it be in point of profit: reputation in them is the last thing to which I shall pretend. I beg pardon for entertaining the reader with so ill a subject; but before I quit that argument, which was the cause of this digression, I cannot but take notice how I am corrected for my quotation of Seneca, in my defence of plays in verse. My words are these: 'Our language is noble, full, and significant; and I know not why he who is master of it, may not cloath ordinary things in it as decently as the Latine, if he use the same diligence in his *choice of words*. One would think, *unlock a door*, was a thing as vulgar as could be spoken; yet Seneca could make it sound high and lofty in his Latin:

Reserate clusos regii postes laris.

But he says of me, *That being filled with the precedents of the Ancients, who writ their plays in verse, I commend the thing; declaring our language to be full, noble, and significant, and charging all defects upon the* ill placing of words, *which I prove by quoting Seneca loftily expressing such an ordinary thing as* shutting a door.

Here he manifestly mistakes; for I spoke not of the placing, but of the choice of words; for which I quoted that aphorism of Julius Cæsar:

Delectus verborum est origo eloquentiœ:

but *delectus verborum* is no more Latin for the placing of words, than *reserate* is Latin for *shut the door*, as he interprets it, which I ignorantly construed *unlock or open* it.

He supposes I was highly affected with the sound of those words; and I suppose I may more justly imagine it of him; for if he had not been extreamly satisfied with the sound, he would have minded the sense a little better.

But these are now to be no faults; for ten days after his book is published, and that his mistakes are grown so famous that they are come back to him, he sends his *Errata*[*] to be printed, and annexed to his play; and desires, that instead of *shutting* you would read *opening*; which, it seems, was the printer's fault. I wonder at his modesty, that he did not rather say it was Seneca's, or mine; and that in some authors, *reserare* was to *shut* as well as to *open*, as the word *barach*[n], say the learned, is both to *bless* and *curse*.

Well, since it was the printer, he was a naughty man to commit the same mistake twice in six lines: I warrant you *delectus verborum* for *placing of words* was his mistake too, though the author forgot to tell him of it: if it were my book, I assure you I should. For those rascals ought to be the proxies of every gentleman author, and to be chastised for him, when he is not pleased to own an errour. Yet since he has given the *Errata*, I wish he would have inlarged them only a few sheets more, and then he would have spared me the labour of an answer: for this cursed printer is so given to mistakes, that there is scarce a sentence in the Preface without some false grammar or hard

[*] This *erratum* has been suffered to remain in the edition of the knight's plays now before us, published in 1692. (Scott.)

sense in it; which will all be charged upon the poet, because he is so good-natured as to lay but three errours to the printer's account, and to take the rest upon himself, who is better able to support them. But he needs not apprehend that I should strictly examine those little faults, except I am called upon to do it: I shall return therefore to that quotation of Seneca, and answer, not to what he writes, but to what he means. I never intended it as an argument, but only as an illustration of what I had said before concerning the election of words: and all he can charge me with is only this,—that if Seneca could make an ordinary thing sound well in Latin by the choice of words, the same, with the like care, might be performed in English: if it cannot, I have committed an errour on the right hand, by commending too much the copiousness and well-sounding of our language; which I hope my countrymen will pardon me. At least the words which follow in my Dramatique Essay will plead somewhat in my behalf; for I say there, that this objection happens but seldom in a play; and then too either the meanness of the expression may be avoided, or shut out from the verse by breaking it in the midst.

But I have said too much in the defence of verse; for after all, it is a very indifferent thing to me, whether it obtain or not. I am content hereafter to be ordered by his rule, that is, to write it sometimes, because it pleases me; and so much the rather, because he has declared that it pleases him. But he has taken his last farewell of the Muses, and he has done it civilly, by honouring them with the name of *his long acquaintances*; which is a complement[1] they have scarce deserved from him. For my own part, I bear a share in the publick loss; and how emulous soever I may be of his fame and reputation, I cannot but give this testimony of his style,—that it is extream poetical, even in oratory; his thoughts elevated sometimes above common apprehension; his notions politick and grave, and tending to the instruction of princes, and reformation of states; that they are abundantly interlaced with variety of fancies, tropes, and figures,

[1] sic.

which the criticks have enviously branded with the name of obscurity and false grammar.

Well, he is now fettered in business of more unpleasant nature: the Muses have lost him, but the commonwealth gains by it; the corruption of a poet is the generation of a statesman.

He will not venture again into the civil wars of censure; ubi... nullos habitura triumphos[n] : if he had not told us he had left the Muses, we might have half suspected it by that word, *ubi*, which does not any way belong to them in that place; the rest of the verse is indeed Lucan's; but that *ubi*, I will answer for it, is his own. Yet he has another reason for this disgust of Poesie; for he says immediately after, that *the manner of plays which are now in most esteem, is beyond his power to perform*: to perform the manner of a thing, I confess is new English to me. *However, he condemns not the satisfaction of others; but rather their unnecessary understanding, who, like Sancho Pança's doctor, prescribe too strictly to our appetities; for, says, he, in the difference of* Tragedy *and* Comedy, *and of* Farce *itself, there can be no determination but by the taste, nor in the manner of their composure.*

We shall see him now as great a critick as he was a poet; and the reason why he excelled so much in poetry will be evident, for it will appear to have proceeded from the exactness of his judgment. *In the difference of Tragedy, Comedy, and Farce itself, there can be no determination but by the taste.* I will not quarrel with the obscurity of his phrase, though I justly might; but beg his pardon if I do not rightly understand him: if he means, that there is no essential difference betwixt comedy, tragedy, and farce, but what is only made by the people's taste, which distinguishes one of them from the other, that is so manifest an errour, that I need not lose time to contradict it. Were there neither judge, taste, nor opinion in the world, yet they would differ in their natures; for the action, character, and language of tragedy, would still be great and high; that of comedy lower and more familiar; admiration would be the delight of one, and satyr[n] of the other.

I have but briefly touched upon these things, because, whatever his words are, I can scarce imagine, that *he who is always concerned for the true honour of reason, and would have no spurious issue fatharerd upon her*, should mean anything so absurd as to affirm, *that there is no difference betwixt comedy and tragedy, but what is made by the taste only*: unless he would have us understand the comedies of my Lord L[*][n], where the first act should be pottages, the second Fricassees, &c. and the fifth a *chére entiére* of women.

I rather guess he means, that betwixt one comedy or tragedy and another, there is no other difference but what is made by the liking or disliking of the audience. This is indeed a less errour than the former, but yet it is a great one. The liking or disliking of the people gives the play the denomination of good or bad; but does not really make or constitute it such. To please the people ought to be the poet's aim, because plays are made for their delight; but it does not follow that they are always pleased with good plays, or that the plays which please them are always good. The humour of the people is now for comedy; therefore, in hope to please them, I write comedies rather than serious plays; and so far their taste prescribes to me: but it does not follow from that reason, that comedy is to be preferred before tragedy in its own nature; for that which is so in its own nature cannot be otherwise; as a man cannot but be a rational creature: but the opinion of the people may alter, and in another age, or perhaps in this, serious plays may be set up above comedies.

This I think a sufficient answer: if it be not, he has provided me of an excuse; it seems, in his wisdom, he foresaw my weakness, and has found out this expedient for me, *That it is not necessary for poets to study strict reason; since they are so used to a greater latitude than is allowed by that severe*

[*] I suppose lord Lauderdale. He was not created a duke till 1672. (Malone.)

inquisition, that they must infringe their own jurisdiction, to profess themselves obliged to argue well.

I am obliged to him for discovering to me this back-door; but I am not yet resolved on my retreat: for I am of opinion that they cannot be good poets, who are not accustomed to argue well. False reasonings and colours of speech are the certain marks of one who does not understand the stage; for moral truth is the mistress of the poet, as much as of the philosopher. Poesie must resemble natural truth, but it must *be* ethical. Indeed the poet dresses truth, and adorns nature, but does not alter them:

Ficta voluptatis causa sint proxima veris[n].

Therefore, that is not the best poesy, which resembles notions of things that are not to things that are: though the fancy may be great, and the words flowing, yet the soul is but half satisfied when there is not truth in the foundation. This is that which makes Virgil be preferred before the rest of Poets: in variety of fancy and sweetness of expression, you see Ovid far above him; for Virgil rejected many of those things which Ovid wrote. *A great wit's great work is to refuse*, as my worthy friend, Sir John Berkenhead[n], has ingeniously expressed it: you rarely meet with anything in Virgil but truth, which therefore leaves the strongest impression of pleasure in the soul. This I thought myself obliged to say in behalf of Poesie; and to declare, though it be against myself, that when poets do not argue well, the defect is in the workman, not in the art.

And now I come to the boldest part of his discourse, wherein he attacques not me, but all the ancients and moderns; and undermines, as he thinks, the very foundations on which Dramatique Poesie is built. I could wish he would have declined that envy which must of necessity follow such an undertaking, and contented himself with triumphing over me in my opinions of verse, which I will never hereafter dispute with him; but he must pardon me, if I have that veneration for Aristotle, Horace, Ben Johnson, and Corneille, that I dare not serve him in such a cause, and against such heroes, but rather fight under their protection, as Homer reports of little Teucer, who shot the Trojans from under the large buckler of Ajax Telamon:

> ΣτΖ δ'αῤ ὑπ' Αἴαντος σα'κεϊ Τελαμωνιαδαο[n].

> He stood beneath his brother's ample shield,
> And cover'd there, shot death through all the field,

The words of my noble adversary are these:

But If we examine the general rules laid down for plays by strict reason, we shall find the errours equally gross; for the great foundation which is laid to build upon, is nothing, as it is generally stated, as will appear upon the examination of the particulars.

These particulars, in due time, shall be examined: in the mean while, let us consider what this great foundation is, which he says is nothing, as it is generally stated. I never heard of any other foundation of Dramatique Poesie than the imitation of nature; neither was there ever pretended any other by the ancients, or moderns, or me, who endeavour to follow them in that rule. This I have plainly said in my definition of a play; that it is a just and lively image of human nature, &c. Thus the foundation, as it is generally stated, will stand sure, if this definition of a play be true; if it be not, he ought to have made his exception against it, by proving that a play is not an imitation of nature, but somewhat else which he is pleased to think it.

But it is very plain, that he has mistaken the foundation for that which is built upon it, though not immediately: for the direct and immediate consequence is this; if nature be to be imitated, then there is a rule for imitating nature rightly; otherwise there may be an end, and no means conducing to it. Hitherto I have proceeded by demonstration; but as our divines, when they have proved a Deity, because there is order, and have inferred that this Deity ought to be worshipped, differ afterwards in the manner of the worship; so, having laid down that nature is to be imitated, and that proposition proving the next, that then there are means which conduce to the imitating of nature, I dare proceed no farther positively; but have only laid down some opinions of the ancients and moderns, and of my own, as means which they used, and which I thought probable for the attaining of that end. Those means are the same which may antagonist calls the foundations, —how properly, the world my judge; and to prove that this is his meaning, he clears it immediately to you, by enumerating those rules or propositions against which he makes his particular exceptions,—as namely, those of time, and place,—in these words: *First, we are told the plot should not be so ridiculously contrived, as to crowd two several countries into one stage; secondly, to cramp the accidents of many years or days into the representation of two hours and an half; and lastly, a conclusion drawn, that the only remaining dispute is, concerning time, whether it should be contained in twelve or twenty-four hours; and the place to be limited to that spot of ground where the play is supposed to begin: and this is called nearest nature; for that is concluded most natural which is most probable, and nearest to that which it presents.*

Thus he has only made a small mistake of the means conducing to the end, for the end itself; and of the superstructure for the foundation: but he proceeds: *To Shew, therefore, upon what ill grounds they dictate laws for Dramatique Poesie, &c.* He is here pleased to charge me with being magisterial, as he has done in many other places of his Preface. Therefore in vindication of myself, I must crave leave to say, that my whole discourse was sceptical, according to that way of reasoning which was used by Socrates, Plato, and all the Academicques of old, which Tully and the best of the ancients followed, and which is imitated by the modest inquisitions of the Royal Society. That it is so, not only the name will shew, which is, *An Essay*, but the frame and composition of the work. You see, it is a dialogue sustained by persons of several opinions, all of them left doubtful, to be determined by the readers in general; and more particularly defer'd to the accurate judgment of my lord Buckhurst, to whom I made a dedication of my book. These are my words in my Epistle, speaking of the persons whom I introduced in my dialogue: It is true, they differed in their opinions, as it is probable they would; neither do I take upon me to reconcile, but to relate them, leaving your lordship to decide it in favour of that part which you shall judge most reasonable. And after that, in my Advertisement to the Reader, I said this: The drift of the ensuing discourse is chiefly to vindicate the honour of our English writers from the censure of those who unjustly prefer the French before them. This I intimate, lest any should think me so exceeding vain, as to teach others an art which they understand much better than myself[n]. But this is more than necessary to clear my modesty in that point; and I am very confident that there is scarce any man who has lost so much time as to read that trifle, but will be my compurgator as to that arrogance whereof I am accused. The truth is, if I had been naturally guilty of so much vanity as to dictate my opinions, yet I do not find that the character of a positive or self-conceited person* is of such advantage to any in this age, that I should labour to be publickly admitted of that order.

But I am not now to defend my own cause, when that of all the ancients and moderns is in question: for this gentleman, who accuses me of arrogance, has taken a course not to be taxed with the other extream of modesty. Those propositions which are laid down in my discourse, as helps to the better imitation of nature, are not mine, (as I have said,) nor were ever pretended so to be, but derived from the authority of Aristotle and Horace,

* Sir Robert Howard's own character. He is supposed to have been ridiculed under the character of Sir *Positive Atall*, in Shadwell's *Sullen Lovers*, represented and published in the same year in which this piece was written. (Malone.) Sir Positive is, adds Scott, 'a foolish knight that pretends to understand everything in the world, and will suffer no man to understand anything in his company; so foolishly positive that he will never be convinced of an error, though ever so gross.' Cf. p. 80, l. 8.

and from the rules and examples of Ben Johnson and Corneille. These are the men with whom properly he contends, and against *whom he will endeavour to make it evident, that there is no such thing as what they all pretend.*

His argument against the unities of place and time, is this: *That it is as impossible for one stage to present two rooms or houses truly, as two countries or kingdoms; and as impossible that five hours or twenty-four hours should be two hours, as that a thousand hours or years should be less than what they are, or the greatest part of time to be comprehended in the less: for all of them being impossible, they are none of them nearest the truth or nature of what they present; for impossibilities are all equal, and admit of no degree.*

This argument is so scattered into parts, that it can scarce be united into a syllogism; yet, in obedience to him, *I will abbreviate* and comprehend as much of it as I can in few words, that my answer to it may be more perspicuous. I conceive his meaning to be what follows, as to the unity of place: (if I mistake, I beg his pardon, professing it is not out of any design to play the *Argumentative Poet.*) If one stage cannot properly present two rooms or houses, much less two countries or kingdoms, then there can be no unity of place; but one stage cannot properly perform this: therefore there can be no unity of place.

I plainly deny his minor proposition; the force of which, if I mistake not, depends on this; that the stage being one place cannot be two. This, indeed, is as great a secret, as that we are all mortal*; but to requite it with another, I must crave leave to tell him, that though the stage cannot be two places, yet it may properly represent them, successively, or at several times. His argument is indeed no more than a mere fallacy, which will

* There is here, I believe, a covert allusion to the character in Shadwell's play already mentioned, who in the first scene, addressing Sandford, says, '—betwixt you and I, let me tell you, *we are all mortal*;' in which *wise* remark the author probably had in view Sir Robert Howard's poem 'Against the Fear of Death.' (Malone.)

evidently appear, when we distinguish place, as it relates to plays, into real and imaginary. The real place is that theatre, or piece of ground, on which the play is acted. The imaginary, that house, town, or country, where the action of the *Drama* is supposed to be; or more plainly, where the scene of the play is laid. Let us now apply this to that Herculean[n] argument, *which if strictly and duly weighed, is to make it evident, that there is no such thing as what they all pretend.* It is impossible, he says, for one stage to present two rooms or houses: I answer, it is neither impossible, not improper, for one real place to represent two or more imaginary places, so it be done successively; which in other words is no more than this; That the imagination of the audience, aided by the words of the poet, and painted scenes, may suppose the stage to be sometimes one place, sometimes another; now a garden, or wood, and immediately a camp: which, I appeal to every man's imagination, if it be not true. Neither the ancients nor moderns, as much fools as he is pleased to think them, ever asserted that they could make one place two; but they might hope, by the good leave of this author, that the change of a scene might lead the imagination to suppose the place altered: So that he cannot fasten those absurdities upon this scene of a play, or imaginary place of action, that it is one place, and yet two. And this being so clearly proved, that it is past any shew of a reasonable denial, it will not be hard to destroy that other part of his argument which depends upon it; namely, that it is as impossible for a stage to represent two rooms or houses, as two countries or kingdoms; for his reason is already overthrown, which was, because both were alike impossible. This is manifestly otherwise; for it is proved that a stage may properly represent two rooms or houses; for the imagination being judge of what is represented, will in reason be less chocqu'd[1] with the appearance of two rooms in the same house, or two houses in the same city, than with two distant cities in the same country, or

[1] Malone and Scott read 'choked.'

two remote countries in the same universe. Imagination in a man or reasonable creature is supposed to participate of reason; and when what governs, as it does in the belief of fiction, reason is not destroyed, but misled, or blinded: that can prescribe to the reason, during the time of the representation, somewhat like a weak belief of what it sees and hears; and reason suffers itself to be so hood-winked, that it may better enjoy the pleasures of the fiction: but it is never so wholly made a captive, as to be drawn headlong into a perswasion of those things which are most remote from probability: 'tis in that case a free-born subject, not a slave; it will contribute willingly its assent, as far as it sees convenient, but will not be forced. Now there is a greater vicinity in nature betwixt two rooms than betwixt two houses, betwixt two houses than betwixt two cities, and so of the rest; Reason therefore can sooner be led by Imagination to step from one room into another, than to walk to two distant houses, and yet rather to go thither, than to flye like a witch through the air, and be hurried from one region to another. Fancy and Reason go hand in hand; the first cannot leave the last behind; and though Fancy, when it sees the wide gulph, would venture over as the nimbler, yet it is withheld by Reason, which will refuse to take the leap, when the distance over it appears too large. If Ben Johnson himself will remove the scene from Rome into Tuscany in the same act, and from thence return to Rome, in the scene which immediately follows, Reason will consider there is no proportionable allowance of time to perform the journey, and therefore will chuse to stay at home. So then, the less change of place there is, the less time is taken up in transporting the persons of the drama, with analogy to reason; and in that analogy, or resemblance of fiction to truth, consists the excellency of the play.

For what else concerns the unity of place, I have already given my opinion of it in my *Essay*;—that there is a latitude to be allowed to it,—as several places in the same town or city, or places adjacent to each other in the same country, which may all be comprehended under the larger denomination of one place; yet with this restriction, that the nearer and fewer those imaginary places are, the greater resemblance they will have to truth; and reason, which cannot make them one, will be more easily led to suppose them so.

What has been said of the unity of place, may easily be applied to that of time: I grant it to be impossible, that the greater part of time should be comprehended in the less, that twenty-four hours should be crowded into three: but there is no necessity of that supposition. For as *Place*, so *Time* relating to a play, is either imaginary or real: the real is comprehended in those three hours, more or less, in the space of which the play is represented; the imaginary is that which is supposed to be taken up in the representation, as twenty-four hours more or less. Now no man ever could suppose that twenty-four real hours could be included in the space of three: but where is the absurdity of affirming that the feigned business of twenty-four imagined hours may not more naturally be represented in the compass of three real hours, than the like feigned business of twenty-four years in the same proportion of real time? For the proportions are always real, and much nearer, by his permission, of twenty-four to three, than of four thousand to it.

I am almost fearful of illustrating anything by similitude, lest he should confute it for an argument; yet I think the comparison of a glass will discover very aptly the fallacy of his argument, both concerning time and place. The strength of his reason depends on this, That the less cannot comprehend the greater. I have already answered, that we need not suppose it does: I say not that the less can comprehend the greater, but only that it may represent it: as in a glass or Mirrour of half a yard diameter, a whole room and many persons in it may be seen at once; not that it can comprehend that room or those persons, but that it represents them to the sight.

But the author of *The Duke of Lerma* is to be excused for his declaring against the unity of time; for, if I be not much mistaken, he is an interested person; the time of that play taking up so many years as the favour of the Duke of Lerma continued; nay, the second and third act including all the time of his prosperity, which was a great part of the reign of Philip the Third: for in the beginning of the second act he was not yet a favourite, and before the end of the third was in disgrace. I say not this with the least design of limiting the stage too servilely to twenty-four hours, however he be pleased to tax me with dogmatizing in that point. In my dialogue, as I before hinted, several persons maintained their several opinions: one of them, indeed, who supported the cause of the French poesie, said, how strict they were in that particular; but he who answered in behalf of our nation, was willing to give more latitude to the rule; and cites the words of Corneille himself, complaining against the severity of it, and observing what beauties it banished from the Stage*. In few words, my own opinion is this, (and I willingly submit it to my adversary, when he will please impartially to consider it,) that the imaginary time of every play ought to be contrived into as narrow a compass as the nature of the plot, the quality of the persons, and variety of accidents will allow. In comedy I would not exceed twenty-four or thirty hours: for the plot, accidents, and persons of comedy are small, and may be naturally turned in a little compass: But in tragedy the design is weighty, and the persons great; therefore there will naturally be required a greater space of time in which to move them. And this though Ben Johnson has not told us, yet it is manifestly his opinion: for you see that to his comedies he allows generally but twenty-four hours; to his two tragedies, *Sejanus* and *Catiline*, a much larger time: though he draws both of them into as narrow a compass as he can: For he shews you only the latter end of Sejanus his favour, and the conspiracy of Catiline already ripe, and just breaking out into action.

But as it is an errour on the one side, to make too great a disproportion betwixt the imaginary time of the play, and the real time of its representation; so on the other side, it is an over-sight

* See p. 48

to compress the accidents of a play into a narrower compass than that in which they could naturally be produced. Of this last errour the French are seldom guilty, because the thinness of their plots prevents them from it; but few Englishmen, except Ben Johnson, have ever made a plot with variety of design in it, included in twenty-four hours, which was altogether natural. For this reason, I prefer *The Silent Woman* before all other plays, I think justly; as I do its author, in judgment, above all other poets. Yet of the two, I think that errour the most pardonable, which in too straight a compass crowds together many accidents; since it produces more variety, and consequently more pleasure to the audience; and because the nearness of proportion betwixt the imaginary and real time, does speciously cover the compression of the accidents.

Thus I have endeavoured to answer the meaning of his argument; for as he drew it, I humbly conceive that it was none; as will appear by his propositon, and the proof of it. His proposition was this.

If strictly and duly weighed, it is as impossible for one stage to present two rooms or houses, as two countries or kingdoms, &c. And his proof this: *For all being impossible, they are none of them nearest the truth or nature of what they present.*

Here you see, instead of proof or reason, there is only *petitio principii*: for in plain words, his sense is this; Two things are as impossible as one another, because thay are both equally impossible: but he takes those two things to be granted as impossible which he ought to have proved such, before he had proceeded to prove them equally impossible: he should have made out first, that it was impossible for one stage to represent two houses, and then have gone forward to prove that it was as equally impossible for a stage to present two houses, as two countries.

After all this, the very absurdity to which he would reduce me is none at all: for he only drives at this, That if his argument be true, I must then acknowledge that there are degrees in impossibilities, which I easily grant him without dispute: and if I mistake not, Aristotle and the School are of my opinion. For there are some things which are absolutely impossible, and others which are only so *ex parte*; as it is absolutely impossible for a thing *to be*, and *not be*, at the same time; but for a stone to move naturally upward, is only impossible *ex parte materiœ*; but it is not impossible for the first mover to alter the nature of it.

His last assault, like that of a Frenchman, is most feeble: for whereas I have observed, that none have been violent against verse, but such only as have not attempted it, or have succeeded ill in their attempt, he will needs, according to his usual custom, improve my observation to an argument, that he might have the glory to confute it. But I lay my observation at his feet, as I do my pen, which I have often employed willingly in his deserved commendations, and now most unwillingly against his judgment. For his person and parts, I honour them as much as any man living, and have had so many particular obligations to him, that I should be very ungrateful, if I did not acknowledge them to the world. But I gave not the first occasion of this difference in opinions. In my Epistle Dedicatory before my *Rival Ladies*, I had said somewhat in behalf of verse, which he was pleased to answer in his Preface to his plays: that occasioned my reply in my Essay; and that reply begot this rejoynder of his in his Preface to *The Duke of Lerma*. But as I was the last who took up arms, I will be the first to lay them down. For what I have here written, I submit it wholly to him; and if I do not hereafter answer what may be objected against this paper, I hope the world will not impute it to any other reason, than only the due respect which I have for so noble an opponent.

NOTES

Preface, viii, 10. Sir Robert Howard (1626-98) was Dryden's brother-in-law. His *Poems* were published in 1660, with verses from Dryden prefixed. In 1665 *Four New Plays of* Howard's were published in folio ; viz. *Surprisal* and *Committee* (comedies), and *Vestal Virgin* and *Indian Queen* (tragedies). The preface of this volume led to Dryden's *Essay* (Ker).

13. [Sir Charles Sedley or Sidley (c. 1639-1701) was about the same age as Dryden. His plays are *Antony and Cleopatra* (1677), a rhyming tragedy, and four others, of which three were comedies. To Sedley is also due one of the most famous and beautiful 'openings' in English poetry:—

> Love still has something of the sea
> From which his mother rose.

He is less favourably known by the story of his wild and dissolute youth which Johnson has recorded in the *Lives of the Poets*.]

16. [The Greeks themselves appear to have had no association of *novus homo* with the name, which conveyed simply the notion of youth and courage. The *Etymologicum Magnum* has *sub voc.*: Ὄνομα κύριον, ἐπεὶ νέος ἀνδρεύσατο ἤ νέος ὢν ἀνδρειος ἦν.]

1. Charles Sackville, Lord Buckhurst, afterwards Earl of Dorset, author of the well-known song 'To all you ladies now on land,' and Lord Chamberlain to William III after the Revolution, was always a kind friend and patron to Dryden, and liberally

assisted him when the loss of his office as poet-laureate, through his refusal to take the oaths to William, brought the poet to great distress. See the long dedication to Dryden's *Discourse concerning the Original and Progress of Satire* (ii.15)[1].

2.15. *The Tragedy of Pompey the Great*, 'translated out of French by certain persons of honour': 4 to 1664. From Dryden's eulogium it appears that the fourth act was translated by Lord Buckhurst; the first was done by Waller (Malone). Sir Charles Sedley, Malone says in another place, had also a hand in this translation, which was from the *Pompée* of Corneille. The act translated by Waller is published among his works.

[*Ibid.* In the second edition of the *Essay* (which is the one here reprinted), Dryden has deliberately eliminated the detached (Sweet, p.138), postponed (Mätzner, ii. 482), or pendent preposition. Instead of 'such arguments as the fourth act of *Pompey* will furnish me with,' he now writes, 'such arguments as those with which the fourth act of *Pompey* will furnish me.' That this change was deliberate appears from Dryden's theory as well as from his practice. In his *Defence of the Epilogue* he enumerates among the weaknesses of Ben Jonson's diction, 'the preposition in the end of the sentence; a common fault with him, and which I have but lately observed in my own writings' (ii.168). Professor Ker's view is that 'in his revision of the *Essay of Dramatic Poesy* Dryden came to believe that he ought to put some restraint on his tendency to leave hanging phrases at the end of his sentences. As he tells us himself, he noted as a fault the preposition left at the end of a clause and belonging to a relative understood' (I.p. xxvii). The most common form of this colloquial use is, of course, that in which there is ellipse of the relative, with the preposition which really governs that relative thrown to the end; but Dryden in revising the *Essay* has also shown himself hostile to the ordinary use of suffixed prepositions, which in

[1] The references to other prose works of Dryden are to Prof. W.P. Ker's edition of the *Essays of John Dryden*, in 2 Vols. (Clarendon Press, 1900).

words like 'allude to', 'deal with,' 'give up,' 'reckon in,' 'sum up,' 'tamper with,' form an integral part of the verbal phrase. The matter is important, as few among the formal points of style more affect the general character of a writer's prose than his fondness for, or avoidance of, these pendent prepositions. In conversation everybody uses them; everybody *says* 'the place he lived in,' no one *says* 'the place in which he lived.' But to use these pendent prepositions in writing as freely as they are used in speech is to leave an over-colloquial and unbraced effect. We all feel, for instance, that considerable though careless writer, Mrs. Oliphant, was ill advised when she penned such a phrase as, '...an offensive hospitality which often annoyed her, and which the Marchioness, for example, scarcely hesitated to show her contempt of' (*At His Gates*, chap. xxvii). On the other hand, to avoid them altogether is perhaps to be over-formal, and to make the gap too wide between the spoken and the written word. In any case, it is interesting to watch the deliberate practice of such a master as Dryden in the following cases, all taken from the *Essay*:—

First Edition	*Second Edition*
P. 12, l. 10, 'The age I live in.'	'The age in which I live.'
P. 24, l. 11,'whom all the story is built upon.'	'on whom the story is built.'
P. 37, l. 22 'tumult which we are subject to.'	'tumult to which we are subject.'
P. 47, l. 10 'end he aimed at.'	'end at which he aym'd.'
P. 77, l. 1 'water which the moon beams played upon	'water, upon which the moon-beams played.'

Apart from these relatival clauses Dryden got rid of the pendent preposition in p. 11, l. 30, where 'hardly dealt with' gives way in the second edition to 'had hard measure'; p. 38, l. 9, where 'all the actor can persuade us to,' becomes 'all the actor can insinuate into us'; p. 41, l. 3, where the second edition eliminates the superfluous 'of' in 'expect to hear of in a sermon'; p. 50, l.5, where 'thrusts him in through a door,' becomes 'thrusts him into a place of safety' (the juxtaposition of the pendent and the normal preposition was here no doubt felt particularly awkward); p. 56, l. 12, where, 'this the poet seems to allude to,' of the first edition, becomes 'to this the poet seems to allude' in the second; and p.65, l. 5, where 'this miserable necessity you are forced upon,' becomes 'you are often forced on this miserable necessity.' We can now see how far Johnson was justified in the assertion (*Life of Dryden*) that 'what he had once written, he dismissed from his thoughts; and I believe there is no example to be found of any correction or improvement made by him after publication. The hastiness of his productions might be the effect of necessity; but his subsequent neglect could hardly have any other cause than impatience of study.' For the whole subject, in addition to Sweet and Mätzner, already cited, see Abbott's *Shakesperian Grammar*, §§ 204 and 424, and Kellner's *Historical Outlines of English Syntax*, pp. 278, 298.]

23. See Valerius Maximus, iv. 5 (*De Verecundia*):—'Excellentis in ea regione (Etruria) pulchritudinis adulescens nomine Spurinna, cum mira specie conplurium feminarum inlustrium sollicitaret oculos ideoque viris ac parentibus earum se suspectum esse sentiret, oris decorem vulneribus confudit deformitatemque sanctitatis suae fidem quam formam inritamentum alienae libidinis esse maluit.'

31. Hor. *Epod.* xvi. 37.

3.4. [This encomium of Charles II's court is probably true as far as dramatic writing is concerned. The critical conferences of St. Evremond, Buckingham, and d'Aubigny early in Charles' reign were probably the beginnings of post-Restoration dramatic criticism. See the first volume of Des Maizeaux' edition of St. Evremond. The king, says Burnet, 'had no literature, but a true and good sense, and had got a right notion of style' (*Elton, Augustan Ages,* p. 201). Cf. Sidney's *Apologie* (Arber, p. 69):—'Undoubtedly I have found in divers smally learned Courtiers a more sound style than in some professors of learning, of which I can guess no other cause but that the Courtier, following that which by practice he findeth fittest to nature, therein (though he know it not) doth according to Art, though not by Art; where the other, using Art to show Art and not to hide

Art (as in these cases he should do) flieth from nature, and indeed abuseth Art.' In the same vein Dryden writes in the *Epistle Dedicatory of the Rival Ladies* (i. 5):—'I have endeavoured to write English, as near as I could distinguish it from the tongue of pedants.' See also this *Essay*, p. 4:—'Only it [this war of opinions] has been prosecuted by some like pedants, with violence of words, and managed by others like gentlemen, with candour and civility'; and p.13.:—'They [the Ancients] can produce nothing so country writ, or which expresses so much the conversation of a gentleman, as Sir John Suckling.' That there was another, and a very serious side, to this Court patronage and to the efforts of writers to obtain it, may be gathered from these lines of Scott (Introduction to *Marmion*):—

> And Dryden in immortal strain
> Had raised the Table Round again,
> But that a ribald King and Court
> Bade him toil on, to make them sport
> Demanded for their niggard pay,
> Fit for their souls, a looser lay,
> Licentious satire, song, and play;
> The world defrauded of the high design,
> Profaned the God-given strength, and marred the lofty line.]

4. To *allow* in the last age signified to approve (Malone). [The *New English Dictionary* explains that the word has two sources, *allaudare* to praise, and *allocare* to bestow, assign. 'The two were apparently completely identified in Old French and viewed as senses of one word, which was adopted with both senses in English before 1300. Between the two primary significations there naturally arose a variety of uses blending them in the general idea of *assign* with *approval*.' For the verb with 'of,' in the sense of *to receive with approval*, the Dictionary quotes Richardson (*Clarissa Harlowe*, 1748). Florio's *Montaigne* (1603) may also be cited (Bk. ii. chap. 12, *init.*): 'Undertaking thenceforward to allow of nothing, except they have first given their voice and particular consent to the same.']

16. I have not, any more than former editors, succeeded in discovering from what French poet these lines are taken. [At my request a French friend has submitted the lines to M. Beljame, whose intimate knowledge alike of the French and of the English literature of the period makes him a good authority. M. Beljame replies that this is not the first time that the lines have been submitted to him. He cannot identify them, and colleagues of his in the University, famous for their knowledge of French seventeenth-century poetry, have been equally unsuccessful. It has been suggested to me from two different French sources (1) that the lines were *vers de société*, handed from salon to salon, but never printed; (2) that Dryden (whose French was probably not equal to such a feat) wrote them himself by way of mystification.]

31. These lines are found in a poem by Sir William Davenant, printed in 4to in 1663, and republished in his works, fol. 1673, p. 268 (Malone).

4. 12. In the *Dedication to The Rival Ladies* [1664]; where Dryden argues for the superiority of rhyme over blank verse.

23. ['Confident of state.' The instances of 'confident' in the sense now reserved for 'confidant,' which are given by the *New English Dictionary*, range from 1647 to 1828. Scott (*Guy Mannering*, chap. ii) wrote:—'As he had neither friend nor confident'; but later editors or printers have unfortunately obscured the matter by substituting 'confidant,' which is now the universal usage. In Dryden's own prose 'confident' recurs in the *Dedication to the Aeneis* (ii. 190)—'Then she was forced to make a confident of her whom she best might trust'; but 'confidant' (unless here also the printers have been at work) in his *Preface to the Translation of Ovid's Epistles* (i. 232)—'Ovid was either the confidant of some other passion.']

28. See Cicero's *Letters to Atticus*, xii. 40, and Plutarch's *Life of Julius Caesar*, chap. liv. 'One of his Dialogues,' *De Finibus*, v. 2.

6. 4. Dryden often uses adjectives as adverbs. In this particular instance he had Shakespeare's example before him. See *Henry VIII*, iv. 2. 52:—

> Exceeding wise, fair-spoken, and persuading.

['Very common in 17-18th cent. now somewhat archaic'—(*New English Dictionary*, which quotes Milton and Wordsworth). See p. 80, 'extream ignorant'; p. 58, 'extreme elaborate.']

7. 13. The engagement between the English and Dutch fleets on June 3, 1665, took place off Harwich. In this memorable battle eighteen large Dutch ships were taken, and fourteen others were destroyed; Opdam, the Dutch admiral, who engaged the Duke of York, was blown up beside him, and he and all his crew perished (Malone). See *Annus Mirabilis*, stanza 22, and Pepys' *Diary* for June 3, 1665:—'3rd. 'All this day by all people upon the river, and almost everywhere else hereabout, were heard the guns, our two fleets for certain being engaged; which was confirmed by letters from Harwich.' Considering the distance of Harwich from London (70 miles by train, of course less as the crow flies), this is an interesting statement.

8. 22. 'Who congratulated to the rest.' The instances given by the *New English Dictionary* of this obsolete construction of the verb range from 1607 to 1710. They include the following from Dryden's dedication to his play of *Aurengzebe*:—'The subjects of England may justly congratulate to themselves....that both our Government and our King secure us from any such Complaint.']

9. 18. This is probably a reference to the Act of 1664, commonly called the Conventicle Act, 'to prevent and suppress seditious and unlawful conventicles.'

28. Cic. *pro Archia*, c. 10.

31. Perhaps the writer first alluded to was Dr. Robert Wild, author of *Iter Boreale*, a panegyric on General Monk, published in April, 1660, and often reprinted; which may be the 'famous poem' alluded to in p. 11. His works were collected and published in a small volume in 1668. The other poet may have been Richard

Flecknoe. Both these poets celebrated the Dutch defeat (Malone).

10.6 'Catachresis' is the improper or abusive use of a word. Cleveland (1613-1658), a 'metaphysical' poet, who abounded in far-fetched images and metaphors, was also the most vigorous satirist on the Cavalier side. Cf. pp. 27, 28, and the following from Cleveland's lines to the *Lycidas* of Milton (Mr. Edward King):—

> I like not tears in tune, nor do I prize
> His artificial grief, who scans his eyes.

28. Martial, *Epigr*. viii. 19.

11.17. George Wither, probably because he was a Puritan and had risen to be major under Cromwell, was the mark for much malicious satire on the part of Tory and Royalist poets. They give him no credit for the lovely lyrical pieces which are for ever associated with his name. Butler (*Hudibras*, Part I, canto i), addressing the Puritanic muse, says:—

> Thou that with ale, or viler liquors,
> Didst inspire Withers, Prynne, and Vickars.

Dryden speaks contemptuously of him in the passage before us, and Pope in the *Dunciad* (i. 296) numbers 'wretched Withers' among 'the dull of ancient days.'

22. 'Auction by inch of Candle, is when, a piece of candle being lighted, people are allowed to bid while it burns, but as soon as extinct, the commodity is adjudged to the last bidder' (Chambers' *Dictionary*). At land sales in France this practice is still in force.

28. Virgil, *Ecl*. iii. 90.

12.4 Petronius Arbiter, Satirae, cap ii.

18. Hor. *Epist*. ii. I. 76

21 Ibid. 34.

13. 12. 'Epic....way.' Whether Dryden meant to include Milton or to ignore him, it is in any case to be borne in mind that *Paradise Lost* was published in 1667, the year before the appearance of Dryden's Essay.

21. 'The drama is wholly ours.' Imitated from the phrase of Quintilian, x.93: 'Satira quidem tota nostra est,' quoted by Dryden in his *Original and Progress of Satire* (ii. 53).

22. Malone rejects 'Eugenius his opinion' as 'ungrammatical phraseology,' but says, supporting himself on the authority of Bishop Lowth, that Dryden ought to have written 'Eugeniusis opinion.' [Cf. 'Augustus his palace,' p. 28; 'Horace his art,' p. 16 ; and 'Sandys his translation,' p. 70. On the other hand, p. 19, Dryden has 'Terence's Eunuch,' and 'Chremes's sister'; evidently the usage was still unfixed. Still more was this the case a generation earlier, when in one and the same line (*Discoveries*, p. 133, Dent) Ben Jonson has 'Achilles' armour' and 'Sophocles his *Ajax*.' In the same way Ben Jonson has 'ass's hoof' (*Ode to Himself*), and Milton has 'ass's jaw' (so in modern editions, but Milton himself spelt 'asses,' as also did Sidney at the end of his *Apologie*), but also 'Glaucus' spell.' 'In Early Modern English the apostrophe was at first intended only to show contraction of *-es*, and was accordingly used freely in the plural as well as the genitive inflexion... The gradual restriction of the apostrophe to the genitive apparently arose from the belief that such a genitive as *prince's* in *the prince's book* was a shortening of *prince his*, as shown by such spellings as *the prince his book*. This belief and this spelling arose very naturally from the fact that *prince's* and *prince his* had the same sound, weak *his* having dropped its 'h' in such collocations, even in the Old English period' (Sweet, *New English Grammar*, i. 321). Mätzner (*English Grammar*, English translation, i. 242-3) discusses the inflected Old-English forms in *es, is,* and *ys*, and on pp. 296-7 has the following about the 'his':—'The connexion of the possessive pronoun of the third person (his) with a substantive, especially a proper name, in the genitive, in which the inflection is then usually wanting, is peculiar: "In characters as red as Mars his heart" (Shakespeare, *Troilus and Cressida*, v. 2), "For Jesus Christ his sake" (*English Liturgy*). Strange to say, in the seventeenth century, as some English grammarians

do even now, the *s* of the genitive was derived from this.... Although the subjoined pronoun in this case makes the inflection of the substantive superfluous, it is originally nothing else than a pleonastic repetition of the substantive notion by the pronoun, which is especially familiar to Old-English in the personal pronoun: "And there Sir Gawaine he her wed" (*Percy Reliques*). "The tanner he took his good cowhide" (*Ibid.*).']

14.20. It is not perfect, because it does not include a *differentia*, and is therefore too wide; it is applicable to epic and heroic poems, and to romances, equally with plays. 'It gives the *general* class (genere) to which a play belongs, and the end (*fine*) which it serves' (Ker). [Cf. p. 71. l. 17: 'For though tragedy be justly preferred above the epic poem, yet there is a great affinity between them, as may easily be discovered in that definition of a play which Lisideius gave us. The *genus* of them is the same—a just and lively image of human nature, in its actions, passions, and traverses of fortune: so is the end—namely, for the delight and benefit of mankind.']

33. See Vell. Paterc. i. 16:—'Una, neque multorum annorum spatio divisa, aetas, per divini spiritus viros, Aeschylum, Sophoclem, Euripidem, illustravit tragoedias: una priscam illam et veterem sub Cratino Aristophane et Eupolide comoediam.' For the construction of 'arrive' with 'to,' cf. p. 39. l. 3.

15. 5, 7. ['Philosophy'=natural science (cf. p. 21, l. 15, and *Original and Progress of Satire* (ii. 34):—'Something new in philosophy and the mechanics is discovered almost every year'); 'Virtuosi'=savants (the singular of the Italian word is used by Evelyn in his *Diary*, February 27, 1644); 'school'=Schoolmen (cf. p. 99, l. 4)]

27. *Historia Romana*, i. 17.

16. 14. ['Remember you.' This obsolete active use of the verb recurs, p.75, II, and *Dedication of the Aeneis* (ii. 188):—'He does wisely to remember you that Virgil,'&c.]

26. Aristotle's treatise on Poetry 'is a fragment, and while

promising to treat of tragedy, comedy, and epic poetry, it treats only of tragedy, adding a few brief remarks on epic poetry, and omitting comedy altogether' (*Encyc .Brit.* 9th ed., art. 'Aristotle'). Περὶ κωμῳδίας ὕστερον ἐροῦμεν wrote Aristotle (Poetics, vi. § i), but the promise was not kept.

28. 'The Three Unities.' The best recent discussion of the Unities is in Prof. Butcher's *Aristotle's Theory of Poetry and Fine Art* (1895), chap. vii. See especially p. 267:—'The only dramatic Unity enjoined by Aristotle is Unity of Action. It is strange that this should still need to be repeated. So inveterate, however, is a literary tradition, once it has been established under the sanction of high authority, that we will find the "Three Unities" spoken of in popular writings as a rule of the *Poetics*.... If Unity of Action is preserved, the other unities will take care of themselves. Unity of Action is indeed in danger of being impaired by marked discontinuity of place or time. There are Spanish dramas in which the hero is born in Act i, and appears again on the scene as an old man at the close of the play. The missing spaces are almost of necessity filled in by the undramatic expedient of narrating what has occurred in the intervals. Yet even here all depends on the art of the dramatist. Years may elapse between successive acts without the unity being destroyed, as we see from *The Winter's Tale* (p. 276)..... French poets and writers on aesthetics did not derive their dramatic rules directly from the Greek models on which the *Poetics* of Aristotle are based. The French, having learnt their three Unities from Roman writers, then sought to discover for them Aristotelian authority. They committed a further and graver error. Instead of resting the minor Unities of Time and Place on Unity of Action, they subordinated Unity of Action to the observance of the other rules. The result not unfrequently was to compress into a space of twelve or twenty-four hours a crowded sequence of incidents and a series of mental conflicts, which needed a fuller development. The natural course of the action was cut short, and the inner consistency of character violated. A similar result

followed from the scrupulous precautions taken to avoid a change of scene. The characters, instead of finding their way to the place where dramatic motives would have taken them, were compelled to go elsewhere, lest they should violate the Unities. The external rule was thus observed, but at the cost of that inward logic of character and events, which is prescribed by the *Poetics*. The failures and successes of the modern stage alike prove the truth of the Aristotelian principle, that Unity of Action is the higher and controlling law of the drama. The unities of Time and Place, so far as they can claim any artistic importance, are of secondary and purely derivative value' (pp. 278-9).

18. 19. ['Corneille calls *la liaison des scènes*.' Cf. Corneille's *Discours des Trois Unités*:—'La liaison des scènes qui unit toutes les actions particulières de chaque acte l'une avec l'autre' (p. 101 'Grands Ècrivains' edition). 'Un acteur occupant une fois le théâtre, aucun, n'y doit entrer qui n'ait sujet de parler à lui. Surtout lorsqu'um acteur entre deux fois dans un acte, il doit absolument ou faire juger qu'il reviendra bientôt quand il sort la premiere fois, ou donner raison en rentrant pourquoi il revient sitôt' (p. 109). Corneille, who bases himself upon Aristotle (ταῦτα δέ δεῖ γίεσθαι ἐξ αὐτZs συστα'σεως τοῦ μὐθουε ὥστε ἐκ τῶν προγεγενημένων σνμβαίνειν ἤ ἐξ a'να'γκης ἤ κara τὸ εἶκος γὶγνεσθαι ταῦτα, *Poetics* x. 3), and Dryden in the above passage, evidently mean a good deal more than that mere avoidance of change of scene within an act, which is all that Dryden means by 'continuity of scenes,' *infra*, p. 55 (cf. pp. 49-50).]

33. See Ben Jonson's *Discoveries*, chap. 135, p. 131 of the 'Temple Classics' edition (Dent, 1898).

19.5. ['There ought to be but one action, says Corneille.' 'Il n'y doit avoir qu'une action complete, qui laisse l'esprit de l'auditeur dans le calme; mais elle ne peut le devenir que par plusieurs autres imparfaites, qui lui servent d'acheminements, et tiennent cet auditeur dans une agreable suspension'(*Discours des Trois Unités*, p. 99).]

23. ['Half-Menander.' In his *Life of Terence*, Suetonius, after quoting Cicero on the poet, goes on:—

Item C. Caesar:—

> Tu quoque, tu in summis, o dimidiate Menander,
> Poneris, et merito, puri sermonis amator.
> Lenibus atque utinam scripts adiuncta foret vis
> Comica, ut aequato virtus polleret honore
> Cum Graecis, neve in hac despectus parte iaceres.
> Unum hoc maceror ac doleo tibi deese, Terenti.

The 'dimidiate' is interpreted by Ritschl in the latest edition of Suetonius' fragments (Reifferscheid) as meaning that, while Menander was equally great as a delineator ἤθη and of πάθη and of (i.e. of character and of passion; see *infra*, p.164), Terence had no command of passion and was a painter of ἤθη only. There is an industrious modern study of Menander, based on the fragments in Meineke's edition (there have been important additions from Egyptian papyri since), by Mr. J. Churton Collins in his *Essays*. What the Greeks felt about him may be gathered from the phrase of Plutarch that 'one could do better without wine than without Menander.']

24. 'Varius.' See Horace, *Od.* i ; *Sat.* i. 9. 23; 10. 44; Ars *Poetica*, 55; Martial, viii 18.5. Nothing in Velleius.

20.5 Macrobius (c. end of fourth century A.D.) wrote *Saturnalia* and two books of commentaries on Cicero's *Somnium Scipionis*. Virgil is discussed in both—at great length in the former.

21. 26. *Historia Romana*, ii. 92.

22. 4. [The division which Dryden ascribes to Aristotle is not in Aristotle's *Poetics*, nor is it to be found in any extant Greek grammarian. The first known instance of it is in the tractate *De tragoedia et comoedia*, printed in Giles' *Terence*, p. xvi, and probably by the Latin grammarian Euanthius. It reappears in J.C. Scaliger's *Poetice*, i. 9. p. 36 of edition of 1586:—'*Protasis* est in qua proponitur et narratur summa rei sine declaratione exitus... *Epitasis* in qua turbae aut excitantur aut intenduntur.

Catastasis est vigor ac status fabulae, in qua res miscetur in ea fortunae tempestate in quam subducta est. *Catastrophe*, conversio negotii exagitati in tranquillitatem non expectatam.']

11. ['The counter-turn.' Cf. p. 50. 21:—'Any quick turns and counterturns of plot,' and Dryden's Notes on Rapin (in Johnson's *Life of Dryden*):—'For the fable itself, 'tis in the English more adorned with episodes, and larger than in the Greek poets; consequently more diverting. For if the action be but one, and that plain, without any counterturn of design or episode (i.e. underplot), how can it be so pleasing as the English, which have both underplot and a turned design, which keeps the audience in expectation of the catastrophe? whereas in the Greek poets we see through the whole design at first.']

17. [In a brawling article on the first edition of this book (Nov. 24, 1894), the *Saturday Review*, not content with the discovery of a blunder in the editor's Englishing of Corneille's *Polyeucte* (though Corneille's *Pompèe* was also Englished in the same line without evoking complaint, and though M. Beljame has Gallicized the titles of Dryden's and other English plays throughout his well-known book), has been bold enough to accuse Dryden himself of an 'amazing blunder on p. 28, where he identifies the λύσις of a tragedy with the Catastrophe.' The only blunder is the Reviewer's. The passage in Aristotle (*Poetics*, xviii. I.) runs thus in the best recent edition (Bywater) of the Greek:—"Εστι δὲ πα'σης τραγῳδίας τὸ μὲν δέσις τὸ δὲ λύσις, τα' μὲν ἔξωθεν καὶ ἔνια τῶν ἔσωθεν πολλα'κις ἡ δέσις, τὸ δὲ λοιπὸν ἡ λύσις—λέγω δὲ δέσιν μὲν εἶναι τὴν α'π' α'ρκZς μέκρι τούτον τοῦ μέρους ὅ ἒσκατόν ἐστιν ἐξ οὗ μεταβαίνειν ει's ετ'τυκίαν....,λύσιν δὲ τὴν α'πὸ τZς α'ρκZς μεταβα'σεως μέκρι τέλοὶς,...πολλοὶ δὲ πλέξαντες εὗ λύουσι καῶς· δεῖ δὲ α'μφω α'εὶ κρατεῖσθαι. Butcher translates as follows:—'Every tragedy falls into two parts—Complication and Unravelling, or *Dénouement*. Incidents extraneous to the action are frequently combined with a portion of the action proper to

form the Complication; the rest is the Unravelling. By the Complication I mean all that comes between the beginning of the action and the part which marks the turning-point from bad fortune to good (or good fortune to bad). The Unravelling is that which comes between the beginning of the change and the end.... Many poets tie the knot well, but unravel it ill. Both arts, however, should always be mastered.' Corneille translates δέσις and λύσις by *nœud* and *dénouement* throughout. There can be no doubt in fact that λύσις means *dénouement*. But can *dénouement* mean Catastophe? It would seem that the Reviewer denies that it can. He must mean that if he means anything. Apparently he has been misled by the geological connotation of the term, and imagines that in the language of the stage also it can only mean one overwhelming act—the arrest of Cinna, for instance, but not the whole *dénouement*, including both the arrest and the subsequent forgiveness. It is easy to show that it is not so. Johnson defines Catastrophe as 'the change or revolution which produces the conclusion and final event of a dramatic piece.' 'The *dénouement*,' adds the *New English Dictionary*. 'The catastrophe or the *dénouement*,' writes J.A. Symonds (*Ben Jonson*, p. 89). Scaliger's definition is 'Conversio negotii exagitati in tranquillitatem non expectatam'—clearly not an act, but a process. Corneille (*Premier Discours*) gives the title of 'Catastrophe' to Clytemnestra's murder of her husband with impunity. The 'impunément' shows that it is the whole *dénouement* he has in view. Still more plainly does this appear from the injunction to keep back 'all the catastrophe' for the fifth act. That phrase, 'toute la catastrophe,' is conclusive as to Corneille's interpretation of the word. The usage of Ben Jonson (*Magnetic Lady*, Interlude between first and second act) is similar:—'Do you look, Master Damplay, for conclusions in a protasis? I thought the law of comedy had reserved them to the catastrophe.']

29. Horace's line is:—

'Neve minor, new sit quinto productior actu.'

Ars Poet. 189. Horace lays it down as a rule applicable to all plays, not comedies only.

22.34 The term 'Jornada' was introduced into Spain by the dramatist Naharro early in the sixteenth century. It is equivalent to day's work, or day's journey. 'The old French mysteries were divided into *journées* or portions, each of which could conveniently be represented in the time given by the Church to such entertainments on a single day. One of the mysteries in this way required forty days for its exhibition' (Ticknor, *Spanish Literature*, i. 270, *note*). [The term therefore did not originally mean *Act*; but Naharro divided his comedies into five jornadas, and with the Spanish dramatists of the next generation the rule was three. In his *Troisiéme Discours*, Corneille says of the number of acts:—'Aristote n'en prescrit point le nombre; Horace le borne à cinq; et, bien qu'il défende d'y en mettre moins, les Espagnols s'opiniâtrent à l'arrêter à trois, et les Italiens font souvent la même chose.' In a note to this passage Voltaire, who was bound to find a reason for everything, found a reason for five acts:—'Cinq actes nous paraissent nécessaires: le premier expose le liew de la scéne, la situation des héros de la pièce, leurs intéerê, leurs moeurs, leurs desseins; le second commene l'intrigue; elle se noue au troisième prépare le dénoûment, qui se fait au cinquième. Moins de temps précipiterait trop l'action; plus d'étendue l'énerverait.' As to three acts, in the Preface to his *Albion and Albanius* (i. 279), Dryden says:—'It is divided, according to the plain and natural method of every nation, into three parts. For even Aristotle himself is contended to say simply that in all actions there is a beginning, a middle, and an end; after which model all the Spanish plays are built.']

23. 7. τὸ μυθός. This is a singular slip; it should of course be ὁ μῦθος.

13. ['Talkative Greeklings.' Juvenal, iii. 78:—'Omnia novit Graeculus esuriens; in caelum, iusseris, ibit.' Cicero, *de Orat.* i. 22, 102:—'Tanquam alicui Graeculo otioso loquaci.' Ben

Jonson, *Discoveries*, p. 123 (Temple Classics):—'I am not of that opinion to conclude a poet's liberty within the narrow limits of laws which either the grammarians or philiosophers prescribe.... Which of the Greeklings durst ever give precepts to Demosthenes?']

24. 'Good cheap' is meant for a literal translation of *bon marché*. Cp. Florio's *Montaigne*, bk. ii, chap. 12:—'The men that serve us do it better cheap.'

34. Terence, *Andria*, iii. i. 15.

24. 3. 'Machine.' [The *deus ex machinâ*, who was let down upon the stage in a chariot or some such contrivance, in order to save the situation at the critical moment. Frequent in Euripides. See the last line of the passage from the Prologue to Jonson's *Every Man in his Humour*, quoted in the note to p. 62, l. 9:—

> Nor creaking throne comes down the boys to please.

'Ces dénoûments par des dieux de machine sont fort fréquents chez les Grecs,' writes Corneille (*Second Discours*). And again:—'Dans le dénoûment, je trouve deux choses à éviter, le simple changement de volonté, et la machine... La machine n'a pas plus d'adresse quand elle ne sert qu'à faire descendre un dieu pour accommoder toutes choses, sur le point que les acteurs ne savent plus comment les terminer' (*Troisième Discours*). 'Oh, how convenient,' says Dryden (*Dedication of the Aeneis*, ii. 189), 'is a machine sometimes in a heroic poem. This of Mercury is plainly one.' Again (*ibid.* 190):—'Of Venus and Juno, Jupiter and Mercury, I say nothing; for they were all machining work.' Once more (*ibid.* 190):—'As for the death of Aruns, who was shot by a goddess, the machine was not altogether so outrageous as the wounding Mars and Venus by the sword of Diomede.']

33. Scaliger, *Poet.* vi. 3, p. 768 (ed. 1586):—'Hoc primum obiiciebant: alterum hoc. Vasta, inquiunt, hians, atque inanis Comoedia est; tota namque intercedit nox. Nam per initia cenam curant; postea Chremes ait, *lucescit.* Sane igitur abiit nox. Haec est illorum obiectio: quam sic diluimus—Datam actamque fa-

bulam ludis Megalensibus. Itaque dimidium fabulae actum vesperi; noctem transactam ludis: alterum dimidium reliquum sub lucem: unam igitur quasi duas.' Sidney *Apologie*, p. 64 (Arber), repeats this explanation, but in mistake substitutes the *Eunuchus* for the *Heautontimorumenos*:—'Yet will some bring in an exmple of *Eunuchus* in Terence, that containeth matter of two days.... True it is, and so was it to be played in two days, and so fitted to the time it set forth.']

25. 3. The *Supplices*. 'This is all from Corneille, Troisième Discours' (Ker.). [For the occasion and the subject-matter of these famous *Discourses*, see Corneille's letter to the Abbé de Pure—Aug.25, 1660—(x. 485 of the 'Grands Ecrivains' edition):—

> 'Je suis à ia fin d'um travail fort pénible sur une matière fort délicate. J'ai traité en trois préfaces les principles questions de l'art poétique sur mes trois volumes de comédies. J'y ai fait quelques explications nouvelles d'Aristote, et avancé quelques propositions et quelques maximes inconnues à nos ancient. J'y réfute celles sur lesquelles I'Académie a fondé la condamnation du *Cid*, et ne suis pas d'accord avec M. d'Aubignac de tout le bien même qu'il a dit de moi. Quand cela paraîtra, je ne doute point qu'il ne donne matière aux critiques: prenez un peu ma protection. Ma première préface exmine si l'utilité ou le plaisir est le but de la poésie dramatique; de quelles utilités elle est capable, et quelles en sont les parties, tant intégrales, comme le sujet et les moeurs, que de quantité, comme le prologue, l'épisode et l'exode. Dans la seconde, je traite des conditions du sujet de la belle tragédie; de quelle qualité doivent être les incidents qui la composent, et les personnes qu'on y introduit, afin d'exciter la potié et la crainte; comment se fait la purgation des passions par cette pitié et cette crainte, et des moyens de traiter les choses selon le vraisemblable ou le nécessaire. Je parle, en la troisiè, des trois unités: d'action, de jour et de lieu. Je crois qu'aprés cela il n'y a plus guère de question d'importance à remuer, et que ce qui reste n'est que la broderie qu'y peuvent ajouter la rhétorique, la morale at la politique.... Vous n'y trouverez pas grande élocution ni grande doctrine; mais. avec tout cela, j'avoue que ces trois préfaces m'ont plus coûté que n'auraient fait trois pièces de thèâtre. J'oubliais de vous dire que je ne prends d'examples modernes que chez moi.'

All three Discourses were published for the first time in 1660, and were consequently quite fresh in people's minds when Dryden composed his *Essay*.]

16. [Corneille in the *Troisième Discours*. After the reference to Euripides, which Dryden has almost literally translated, Corneille goes on:—'C'est assez bien employé un temps si court.' *Employé* is the reading of all the editions published in Corneille's lifetime.]

26. 3. This reference to Terence comes from Corneille, *Discours des Trois Unités*, p. 102.

27. 3 The satyr-drama of the *Cyclops*, by Euripides, a kind of farce, is the only specimen remaining to us of a form of theatrical entertainment to which all the Greek tragedians had recourse in order to relieve the mental tension consequent on witnessing the performance of a long tragedy. There are *elements* of comic treatment in the *Alcestis* and even in the *Antigone*. [In an interesting letter to Goethe (ii. 98 of the English translation of their Correspondence) Schiller complains of 'a kind of playfulness in the serious dialogues of Sophocles.' In a defence of Tragi-comedy published in 1648, Ogier relied chiefly on the *Cyclops*, which he described as 'une tragi-comédie pleine de raillerie et de vin, de satyres et de silènes d'um côté, de sang et de rage de Polyphème éborgné de l'autre.']

23. Ter. *Eunuchus*, act ii. sc. I. 17, 18.

33. Our author has quoted from memory. The lines are, At *nostri proavi*, etc., and afterwards, *Ne dicam* stulte *mirati* (Malone). Hor. *A.P.* 270.

28.5. Hor. *A. P.* 70

7. Cleveland. See pp. 11, 136.

9. Catachresis; see above p. II, 136.

10. Virg. *Ecl.* iv. 20.

14. Virg. *Aen.* viii. 91.

17. Ovid, *Met* i. 175; and (below) ib 561. Malone says that the true reading is *pompae*, and this is adopted iin Burmann's edition; but *longas... pompas* occurs in the best MSS., and is printed by all recent editors. Malone also points out that in the

preceding quotation, for *verbo* we should read *verbis*, and for *metuam summi, timeam magni.*

29. 4. From *The Rebel Scot*, by Cleveland, l. 61.

7. Juv. *Sat*. x. 123.

10. From Cleveland's *Rupertismus*, 39-40. 'White powder' is arsenic.

26. Ovid, *Tristia*, ii. 381.

30. Our author (as Dr. Johnson has observed) might have determined this question upon surer evidence, for it (*Medea*) is quoted by Quintilian (ix. 2. 8) as Seneca's, and the only line which remains of Ovid's play, for one line is left us, is not found there (Malone). Ovid's line, cited by Quintilian (viii. 5. 6), as stronger and more impressive than the adage *Nocere facile est, prodesse difficile*, is—*Servare potni; perdere an possim rogas?* [Elsewhere Quintilian (x. i. 98) says of Ovid's play:—'Ovidii Medea videtur mihi ostendere quantum ille vir praestare potuerit, si ingenio suo imperare quam indulgere maluisset.' For the dramatic character of Ovid's genius see Dryden's *Preface to Annus Mirabilis* (i. 15, 16).]

30. 15. Juv. *Sat*. vi. 195.

31. 5. Virg. *Aen.* i. 378; parts of two lines.

14. Hor. *Sat*. x. 68.

19. Horace, *Epist*. ii. I. 49.

32. 18. Pierre Corneille was born at Rouen in 1606, and produced his first play, *Mélite*, a comedy, in 1625.

28. Aristotle, *Poetics*, v. § 8.

33. 16. ['Tis a drama of our own invention.' The assertion is, of course, incorrect. The Tragi-comedy was the specific Spanish form. The most noted example was *La Celestina*, a play of great length, extending to twenty-one acts, and produced between 1480 and 1490. Fernando Rojas was the author of all but the first act. France adopted the form from Spain, and was rated by Voltaire in the following terms for doing so:—

'Lorsque Corneille donna *Le Cid*, les Espagnols avaient, sur tous les thèâtres de l'Europe, la même influence que dans les affaires publiques... II est vrai que, dans presque toutes ces tragédies espagnoles, il y avait toujours quelques scènes de bouffonneries. Cet usage infecta ;'Angleterre. II n'y a guère de tragédies de Shakespeare où l'on ne trouve des plaisanteries d'hommes grossiers à côté du sublime des héros. À quoi attribuer une mode si extravagante et si honteuse pour l'esprit humain qu'à la coutume des princes mêmes qui entretenaient toujours des bouffons auprês d'eux; coutume digne des barbares, qui sentaient le besoin des plaisirs de l'esprit, et qui étaient incapables d'en avoir; contume même qui a duré jusqu'à nos temps, lorsqu'on en reconnaissit la turpitude? Jamais ce vice n'avilit la scène francaise; il se glissa seulement dans nos premiers opéras, qui, n'étant pas des onvrages réguliers, semblaient permettre cette indécence; mais bientôt l'élégant Quinault purgea l'opéra de cette bassesse. Quoi qu'il en soit, on se piquait alors de savior ;'espagnol, comme on se fait honneur aujourd'hui de parler francais. C'était la langue des cours de Vienne, de Bavière, de Bruxelles, de Naples et de Milan: la Ligue l'avait introduite en France, et le mariage de Louis XIII avec ls fille de Phillippe III avait-tellement mis l'espagnol à la mode qu'il était alors presque honteux aux gens de lettres de l'ignorer. La plupart de nos comédies étaient imitées du théâtre de Madrid.' (*Préface Historique de Voltaire sur le Cid, init.*)

Martinenche (*La Comédie espagnole en France*, 1900) quotes several Spanish pleas in favour of the Tragi-comedy, and even suggestes that it paved the way in France for the genius of Molière, 'qui n'est peut-être si grand que parce qu'il a tiré son plus haut comique de la plus tragique des matières'; but he also admits the really vital objection to the Tragi-comedy, or rather to its abuse.

'Nous pouvons admettre (p. 123), si spécial soit-il, le rôle du gracioso, mais comment supporter qu'au beau de la plus tragique situation il lance une grossière plaisanterie? Argensola (1634) le remarquait avec raison, c'est le meilleur moyen de gâter une noble émotion. On a le droit, dans une même oeuvre, de faire appel à des tonalités différentes, mais si on ne les fait point hurler ensemble, si on les fond par des transitions insensibles en une savante harmonie.'

In the same strain Dryden writes at a later period (*Parallel of Poetry and Painting*, ii. 146):—

> 'The Gothic manner, and the barbarous ornaments, which are to be avoided in a picture, are just the same with those in an ill-ordered play. For example, our English tragi-comedy must be confessed to be wholly Gothic, notwithstanding the success which it has found upon our theatre, and in the *Pastor Fido* of Guarini; even though Corisca and the Satyr contribute somewhat to the main action. Neither can I defend my *Spanish Friar*, as fond as otherwise I am of it, from this imputation: for though the comical parts are diverting, and the serious moving, yet they are of an unnatural mingle: for mirth and gravity destroy each other, and are no more to be allowed for decent than a gay widow laughing in a mourning habit.'

Addison does little but repeat this passage in the 40th *Spectator*.]

23. The Red Bull, in St. John's Street, was one of the meanest of our ancient theatres, and was famous for entertainments adapted to the taste of the lower orders of the people (Malone). In Strype's edition of Stow's *London* there is a plan of the parish of St. James, Clerkenwell, on which is marked 'Red Bull Yard,' between St. John's Street and Clerkenwell Green. This must have been the site of the theatre. The ground formerly belonged to the priory of St. John at Jerusalem; and it is not unlikely that, as Shakespeare and his company turned the ruinous buildings of the Blackfriars, near St. Paul's, to account for a theatre, the patrons of the Red Bull made a similar use of the monastic ruins at Clerkenwell. In his *Annals of the Stage* (iii. 324) Mr. Collier collects a number of notices, more or less interesting, of the Red Bull Theatre. Wither, in his Satires, Randolph in his *Muses' Looking Glass*, and Prynne in the *Histriomastix*, all make mention of it. It was pulled down not long after the Restoration, and Drury Lane was regarded as having taken its place.

24. Hor. *Epist.* ii. I. 185. Horace wrote:—

> Si discordet eques, media inter carmina poscunt
> Aut ursum aut pugiles.

26. [‘Admiration.’ Aristotle says nothing of admiration. The famous words are (*Poetics*, 6. § 2):—*δί ἐλέον καὶ φόβου περαίνονσα τὴν τῶν τοιούτων παθημα’των κα’θαρσιν*, ‘through pity and fear effecting the proper purgation of these emotions, (Butcher, after Bernays and Weil). In his Notes on Rapin, Dryden argues that ‘it may admit of doubt whether pity and terror are either the prime, or at least the only ends of tragedy. ‘Tis not enough that Aristotle had said so; for Aristotle drew his models from Sophocles and Euripides; and if he had seen ours might have changed his mind.... If then the encouragement of virtue and discouragement of vice be the proper ends of poetry in tragedy, pity and terror, though good means, are not the only. For all the passions, in their turns, are to be set in a ferment; as joy, anger, love, fear are to used as the poet’s commonplaces; and a general concernment for the principal actors is to be raised, by making them appear such in the characters, their words and actions, as will interest the audience in their fortunes.’ It is remarkable that Dryden anticipated the pathological explanation of Catharsis, which, since Bernays, has been accepted by almost all good authorities; and it would be still more remarkable if Dryden had not been himself anticipated by Milton[1] (in the Preface to *Samson Agonistes*), who was himself anticipated by at least one seventeenth-century Italian, and by Corneille (see the letter to the Abbé de Pure quoted on p. 145). In the *Dedication to the Aeneis* (ii. 258) he writes:—‘To raise, and afterwards to calm the passions—to purge the soul from pride by the examples of human miseries, which befall the greatest—in few words, to expel arrogance and introduce compassion (to “remove pride and hard-heartedness,” *ibid.* 166), are the great effects of tragedy.’ As for ‘admiration,’ Dryden elsewhere seems to regard it as the peculiar effect and object of the *epic*. In the *Dedication of Examen Poeticum* (ii. 12.) he writes:—‘Yet I must needs say this in reference to Homer, that he

[1] See Prof. Bywater’s interesting article on ‘Milton and the Aristotelian Definiion of Tragedy’ in the *Journal of Philology* for 1901, xxvii. 267.)

is much more capable of exciting the manly passions than those of grief and pity. To cause admiration is indeed the proper and adequate design of an Epic Poem; and in that he has excelled even Virgil.' And in *A Parallel of Poetry and Painting* (ii. 243):—'The hero...is the chief object of pity in the drama, and of admiration in the epic poem.' Sidney, however, whose *Apologie* Dryden often had in mind, had written (Arber, p. 65):—'A Comedy should be full of delight, as the Tragedy should be still maintained in a well-raised admiration.']

34. 4. Hor. *Ars Poet.* 240.

12. Ibid. 151.

17. Dryden here used 'success' in the sense of the Spanish *suceso*, which means 'event,' or 'issue' [See his *Original and Progress of Satire* (ii. 51):—'This was the subject of the tragedy; which, being one of those that end with a happy event, is therefore, by Aristotle, judged below the other sort, whose success is unfortunate.']

20. Justin, who probably lived in the age of the Antonines, abridged the *Universal History* of Pompeius Trogus, a contemporary of Livy. The reference here is to Justin, i.8 ('the true Cyrus in Justin,' Sidney, *Apologie* (Arber, p. 36).

22. The writers from whom we learn the story of Cyrus are (besides Justin) Herodotus, Ctesias, and Xenophon. Of these Herodotus, as living nearest to the time, is the most trustworthy. The *Cyropaedia* of Xenophon ('the feigned Cyrus of Xenophon,' Sidney, ibid.) is an historical romance, nor does the writer himself pretend that it is anything more. Herodotus makes Cyrus, when advanced in years, invade the country of the Massagetae, whose queen was Tomyris, and lose his life in battle.

35. 4. Hor. *Ars Poet.* 188.

7. Hesiod, *Theog.* 27; Homer, *Od.* xix. 203.

23. 'Spanish plots.' The chief adaptations from the Spanish drama were *Elvira, or the worst not always True*, by a Person of Quality (the Earl of Bristol), 1667, from Calderon, *No siempre*

lo Peor es cierto; and the *Adventures of Five Hours*, 1663, by sir Samuel Tuke, from *Los Empeños de seis Horas*, attributed to Calderon. Lord Bristol made two other versions from Calderon, which are not extant (Ker). [The plot of Calderon's *Mock Astrologer* (*El Astròlogo Fingido*) was borrowed by Thomas Corneille, and from him by Dryden for his play of that name. But the debt of England, and of Europe generally, to the Spanish stage—chiefly through the medium of France—is by no means limited to these instances. Martinenche quotes Chappuzeau (1674) as saying:—'Les Francis ont su tenir le milieu entre les Italiens et les Espagnols, et par un heureux tempérament se former un *caractére univesal* qui s'éloigne également des deux excès. Mais au fond nous sommes plus obligés aux Espagnols'; and then goes on (p. 425):—

> 'Les Italiens ne nous ont enseigné que leurs *lazzi* superficiels et la fantaisie licencieuse de leurs intrigues. Les Espagnols ne se sont pas contentés de fournir de sujets de scènes l'imagination créatrice de not grands poètes dramatiques. Ils nous ont véritablement ouvert le chemin du théâtre moderne en nous révélant les éternels ressorts de la tragédie et de la comédie. Certes leur conception de l'anour et de l'honneur tenait trop à la mode de leur pays et participait à la cruauté et à l'ardeur spéciales de leurs moeurs. Mais Corneille n'aurait peut-être pas concu sans eux son superbe drame de la volonté et Moliére n'a pas eu à se repentir d'avoir cherché aprés eux le rire à la même source que les pleurs.' See note to .]

25. *The Bloody Brother*, also called *The Tragedy of Rollo Duke of Normandy*, by John Fletcher, was first printed in 1639. The plot is taken from the fourth book of Herodian; it is Roman imperial history transferred to new times, places, and persons; Caracalla and Geta become Rollo and Otto. See A. W. Ward's *Dramatic Literature*, ii. 734-5.

36.1. 'Oleo,' or 'oglio,' is a corruption of *olla in olla podrida*, a Spanish dish consisting of a stew of several kinds of meat and vegetables. *Oleo*, therefore, means a mess or mixture. Cf. *Original and Progress of Satire* (ii. 104):—'That *olla*, or hotch-potch, which is properly a satire.'

34. Dryden appears to have borrowed this word from Corneille, who speaks (*Rodog*. Exam.) of a 'personnage protatique,' i.e. an introductory character; it stands for the Greek προτατικὸν πρόσωπον, which Donatus in his preface to the *Andria* of Terence represents in Latin by 'protatica persona.' ['Pour ouvrir son sujet Térence a introduit une nouvelle sorte de personnages qu'on a appelés protatiques, parce qu'ils ne paraissent que dans la protase, où se doit faire la proposition et l'ouverture du sujet' (Corneille, *Discours du poéme Dramatique*, p. 46). See note to 22. 4]

37. 3. ['Interessed.' Cf. *Original and Progress of Satire* (ii. 33):—'Without interessing Heaven in the quarrel.' *Parallel of Poesy and Painting* (ii. 130):—'By which he gained the hearts of a great nation to interess themselves for Rome against Carthage.' The same French spelling (showing that the word was still comparatively novel) recurs in Dryden's text in the *Preface to Albion and Albanius* (i. 279) and the *Dedication of the Aeneis* (ii. 191). There is an earlier use of the form in Daniel's *Defence of Rhyme* (Grosart's edition of Daniel's complete works, iii. 34, 37). Dryden uses the ordinary modern spelling, p. 96. l. 34, unless indeed the editors have been at work, as they have in the Preface to Dryden's *Religio Laici*, where 'nothing interessed in that dispute' was regularly printed 'interested' till the arrival on the scene of Mr. Christie. In *Religo Laici* itself, l. 333—

> When general, old, disinteressed, and clear,

the editors, including even Scott, have destroyed the metre by printing 'disinterested' for 'disinteressed.']

18. ['Ten or twenty years ago.' See Corneille, *Discours des Trois Unités*, pp.104-105:—'J' ajoute un conseil, de s'embarrasser le moins qu'il lui est possible de choses arrivées avant l'action qui se représente. Ces narrations' (observe this word Englished above,) 'importunent d'ordinaire, parce qu'elles ne sont pas attendues, et qu'elles gènent l'esprit de l'auditeur, qui est oblifé de charger sa mémoire de ce qui s'est fait dix ou

douze ans auparavant, pour comprendre ce qu'il voit représenter; mais celles qui se font des choses qui arrivent et se passent derrière le théâtre, depuis l'action commencée, font toujours un meilleur effet, parce qu'elles sont attendues avec queique curiosité, et font partie de cette action qui se représente.']

25. ['Fight prizes.' In Scott's *Woodstock*, chap. xiv, General Harrison is made to say:—'I have been accounted a master of fence, and have fought prizes when I was unregenerated.' The *New English Dictionary* also quotes Browning, *Paracelsus*, iv. 119, 'while we fight the prize.']

26. Cf. Sidney's *Apologie* (Arber, p. 63) in an argument for Unity of Place:—'Now ye shall have three Ladies walk to gather flowers, and then we must believe the stage to be a Garden. By and by we hear news of shipwreck in the same place, and then we are to blame if we accept it not for a Rock. Upon the back of that comes out a hideous Monster, with fire and smoke, and then the miserable beholders are bound to take it for a Cave. While in the meantime two Armies fly in, represented with four swords and bucklers, and then what hard heart will not receive it for a pitched field?']

38. 10. ['Than all the actor can insinuate into us.' Cf. p. 47:—'Whether custom has so insinuated itself into our courtrymen.' Charles Lamb, who knew his Dryden well, has taken over this verb from our author in a well-known passage:—'The actor must pronounce [these profound sorrows, &c.] *ore rotundo*, he must accompany them with his eye, he must insinuate them into his auditory by some trick of eye, tone, or gesture, or he fails' (*On the Tragedies of Shakespeare*, p. 256).

32. ['Corneille says judiciously.' 'Le poëte n'est pas tenu d'exposer à la vue toutes les actions particulières quiaménent à la principale: il doit choisir celles qui lui sont les plus avantageuses à faire voir, soit par la beauté du spectacle, soit par l'éclat et la véhémence des passions qu'elles produisent, soit par quelque autre agrément qui leur soit attaché, et cacher les autres derriére

la scéne, pour les faire connaitre au spectateur, ou par une narration, ou par quelque autre adresse de l'art' (*Discours des Trois Unités*, p. 100).

39. 20. Hor. *A.P.* 180-7, Horace writes 'Ne pueros': a line is omitted after 'trucidet.'

30. The reference is to act iii. sc. i. 2, of Jonson's comedy of *The Magnetic Lady*.

40. 9. The title of this play, the joint work of Beaumont and Fletcher, and first acted in 1611, was *A King and no King*. In the last act, Gobryas, a noble, reveals to Arbaces, king of Illyria, that he is really his son, and not the son of Arane, the queen mother; Arbaces, thus become a subject and 'no' King,' marries Panthea, the true heir to the throne, and all ends happily.

20. 'Simple change of will.' See the passage from Corneille's Third Discourse, quoted on p. 116, note to 24. 3, and the following from the First Discourse, pp. 27-28:—'Nous devons toutefois prendre garde que ce consentement'(of parents to the marriage of lovers) 'ne vienne pas par un simple changement de volonté, mais par un événement qui en fournisse l'occasion. Autrement il n'y aurait pas grand artifice au dénouement d'une piéce, si, aprés l'avoir soutenue durant quatre actes su l'autorité d'un pére qui n'approuve point les inclinations amoureuses de son fils ou de sa fille, il y consentait tout d'un coup au cinquiéme, par cette seule raison que c'est le cinquiéme, et que l'auteur n'oserait en faire six. Il faut un effort considerable qui l'y oblige, comme si Pamant de sa fille lui sauvait la vie en quelque rencontre où il fût prêt d'être assassiné par ses ennemis, ou que par quelque accident inespéré il fût reconnu pour être de plus grande condition et mieux dans la fortune qu'il ne paraissit.']

28. *The Scornful Lady*, a joint play of Beaumont and Fletcher, was produced sometime before 1609. 'The sudden conversion of the usurer Morecraft is imitated from the *Adelphi* of Terence, where the same change takes place in the character of Demea' (Dyce). See Wards's *Dramatic Literature*, ii. 668.

41. 17. ['Il faut, s'il se peut, y rendre raison de l'entrée et de la sortie de chaque acteur; surtout porr la sortie je tiens cette règle indispensable, et il n'y a rien de si mauvaise grâce qu'un acteur qui se retire du théâtre seulement parce qu'il n'a plus de vers à dire.' Corneille, *Discours des Trois Unités*.]

42. 2. Velleius Paterculus, i. 17.

27. The *Menteur* of Corneille (see Geruzez, Lit. *Française*, ii. 90) was founded on one of the *chefs-d'oeuvre* of the Spanish stage, the *Truth itself Suspected* (*La Verdad Suspechosa*) of Ruiz de Alarcon. It appeared in 1642. Corneille himself wrote of it:—'Ce n'est ici qu'une copie d'un excellent original.'

43. 8. Cardinal Richelieu died in 1642.

11. The *Knight of the Burning Pestle* and *Double Marriage* of Beaumont and Fletcher, which are founded on two of Cervantes' novels, are cases in point. Middelton's *Spanish Gipsy* is from Cervantes (Ker).

13. *The Adventures of Five Hours*, written by Sir Samuel Tuke, and printed in 1663. Diego is a character in it (Malone). See note to 35. 23.

33. 'Contraries are the two most opposite qualities of the same class of subjects, e.g. black and white, as colours of bodies; virtue and vice, as habits of the soul' (Mansel's *Artis Logicae Rudimenta*, 19).

44. 24. The Doctrine of the *primum mobile* belongs to the Ptolemaic astronomy, which made the sun and stars revolve round the earth. 'In the old astronomy the sphere beyond the sphere of the Fixed Stars, which gives to the eight lower spheres their diurnal motion from east to west' (Ker).

45. 23. *Cinna, or the Clemency of Augustus*, produced in 1639, is generally allowed to the Corneille's finest tragedy. [Corneille himself wrote of it in his *Troisième Discours*:—'Une des raisons qui donne tant d'illustres suffrages à *Cinna* pour le mettre au-dessus de ce que j'ai fait, c'est qu'il n'y a aucune narration du passé, &c.; and in a note to the same *Discours* Voltaire says:— 'Il y a quelques défauts de style dans *Cinna*; on

y a découvert aussi quelques fautes dans la condite et dans les sentiments: mais en général il y régne une si noble simplicité, tant de naturel, tant de clarté, le style a tant de beautés, qu'on lira toujours cette piéce avec intérêt et avec admiration.'] On the *Pompée*, see the note on p. 101. The *Polyeucte*, a story of Christian martyrdom referring to the persecution of the Emperor Decius, appeared in 1640. The author's 'Examen, on this play is of great interest.

46. 13. ['Chace of wit.' Apparently from the quick volleys and returns of the game of tennis, in which 'chase' is a familiar technical term; see the *New English Dictionary*.]

47. 3. *The Maid's Tragedy* is by Beaumont and Fletcher; the other plays here mentioned are by Ben Jonson.

48.1. The *Andromède*, from the gorgeousness of its mythological *mise-en-scène*, bore some resemblance to the masque, while from the use of recitative and the introduction of many songs it approached the modern opera. Among the 'dramatis personae' there were only ten human beings against twelve gods and goddesses. The opening scene showed a huge mountain, pierced by a grotto, through which appeared the sea; Melpomene entered on one side, and the Sun on the other, in a 'char tout lumineux,' drawn by four horses.

13. In the north of Etruria, about 180 miles from Rome. See p. 95, l. 23.

20. There is no passage in Ben Jonson's works in which he directly censures Shakespeare for the non-observance of the unities of Time and Place. Dryden can only refer to the Prologue to *Every Man in his Humour*. This Prologue first appeared in 1616, and its intended application to Shakespeare may well have been traditionally known in the theatrical world fifty years later. In it Jonson, among the 'ill customs of the age' which he will not imitate, enumerates—

> To make a child now swaddled to proceed
> Man, and then shoot up, in one beard and weed,
> Past threescore years; or, with three rusty swords,
> And help of some few foot and half-foot words,
> Fight over York and Lancaster's long jars,

And in the trying-house bring wounds to scars.
He rather prays you will be pleased to see
One such to-day, as other plays should be;
Where neither chorus wafts you o'er the seas,
Nor creaking throne comes down the boys to please, &c.

Other dramatists may have included in the censure; but it seems clear that Shakespeare was principally intended, the three parts of whose *Henry VI* (assuming Shakespeare's responsibility for all of them) extend over the events of nearly fifty years, including the whole of 'York and Lancaster's long jars,' whose Perdita is born and grow up to be a woman between the first and fifth acts, and who makes the Chorus in *The Winter's Tale* say—the play having begun in Sicily—

imagine me,
Gentle Spectators, that I now may be
In fair Bohemia.

49. 31. Thomas Corneille's (the younger) *L'Amour à la Mode* (1651), Englished in 1675 as *The Amorous Gallant, or Love in Fashion* (Ker).

50. 9. A servant in Sir Samuel Tuke's *Adventures of Five Hours*, who is described by the author as 'a great coward, and a pleasant droll.' [Philipin is a common name for the comic servant in French imitations from the Spanish. The type of the *gracioso* was taken over by these imitators, and Diego, his regular name in the Spanish originals, became Philipin. 'Les "graciosos" et les "graciosas" sont des types qu'on ne peut transporter tels quels sur la scène étrangère. Mais ils sont autrement modernes at complexes que les esclaves antiques ou les serviteurs de la comédie italienne, et quand on les dépouillera de leur enveloppe espagnole ils auront plus d'une leçon à donner à nos valets et à nos "servantes."... Il en est du "gracioso" comme du choeur antique. Il n'est point une partie éternelle du drame, mais il est indispensable à la comédie particulière où il joue un des principaux rôles. Il est le bon sens qui corrige les folies et les

enthousiasmes, il rappelle la vérité humaine en présence des excés et des monstruosités. Il est le lien indispensable entre l'Espagne chevaleresque et l'Espagne picaresque... S'il faut reconnaître à Scarron le mérite d'avoir acclimaté en France le valet de comédie dont Moliére nous donnera le type achevé, il ne faut pas oublier qu'il nous vient de Rojas et de la comédie ironique, et qu'il est beaucoup plus le fils du gracioso espagnol que du *zanni* italien.' Martinenche, *La Comédie Espagnole en France* (1900) pp. 109, 119, 389.]

51.5 This subject had been imperfectly examined at the time when Dryden wrote, and his statement is not quite accurate. It is true most of the old comedies before Shakespeare, such as *Ralph Roister Doister* and *Gammer Gurton's Needle*, were written in rude twelve-syllable lines; to class these with the elegant French Alexandrines of the period is to pay them much too high a compliment. But there were exceptions; the *Misogonus* of Richards (about 1560) is in fourteen-syllable alternate rhymes; the *Supposes* of Gascoigne (1566) is in prose; and the *Taming of a Shrew* (1594) is in blank verse. See Collier, *Annals of the Stage*. vol. iii. But the chief injustice of Dryden's *obiter dictum* lay in his saying nothing of Lyly, who, as a writer of prose dialogue interspersed with blank verse, is important for his purpose.

10. The unfinished pastoral drama of *The Sad Shepherd*, or *A Tale of Robin Hood*, must have been written not long before Jonson's death in 1637; the prologue opens with the line—

> He that hath feasted you these forty years.

14. The pastoral drama of *The Faithful Shepherdess*, by Fletcher, was published by 1610.

26. Dryden truly says that *The Merry Wives of Windsor* is 'almost exactly formed'; that is, that the unities of time and place are nearly observed. The time of the action is comprised within two days; the place is, either some house in Windsor, or a street in Windsor, or a field near the town, or Windsor Park.

17. ['To return whence I have digressed.' The substitution, of 'whence' for the loose and pleonastic 'from whence' of the first edition, is another proof of the injustice of Johnson's charge against Dryden, that he took no pains to mend his style. (See p. 103) To the instances there given of elimination of needless or pendent prepositions should be added 49.5, where the 'bound up' of the first edition becomes simply 'limited' in the second.]

52. 11. 'It is curious to observe with what caution our author speaks, when he ventures to place Shakespeare above Jonson; a caution which proves decisively the wretched taste of the period when he wrote' (Malone).

27. Virg. *Ecl.* i. 26.

28. John Hales, Fellow of Eton, was a friend of Sir Henry Wotton. The *Golden Remains of the Ever Memorable Mr. John Hales* was published in 1659. There is a story of his being present when Ben Jonson was speaking of Shakespeare's want of learning (Ker).

53. 13. [See Ben Jonson's fifty-fourth Epigram:—

How I do love thee, Beaumont, and thy Muse,
That unto me dost such religion use!
How I do fear myself, that am not worth
The least indulgent thought thy pen drops forth!
At once thou mak'st me happy, and unmak'st,
And giving largely to me, more thou tak'st!
What fate is mine, that so itself bereaves?
What art is thine, that so thy friend deceives?
When even there, where most thou praisest me,
For writing better, I must envy thee.]

14. Chiefly on account of the woman-page Bellario, in whose mouth are put a profusion of pretty and graceful things which might often deserve to have been said by Shakespeare's Viola. Lamb says (*Eng. Dramatic Poets*, p. 308), 'For many years after the date of *Philaster's* first exhibition on the stage [1608], scarce a play can be found without one of those women pages in it, following in the train of some prengaged lover.'

54. 2. Mr. Dyce, in his excellent edition of Beaumont and Fletcher (1844), enumerates the following plays as certainly, or almost certainly, the joint work of the two:—

Philaster.
The Maid's Tragedy.
The Knight of the Burning Pestle.
King and no King.
Cupid's Revenge.
The Coxcomb.
Four Plays in One.
The Scornful Lady.
The Honest Man's Fortune.
The Little French Lawyer.
Wit at several Weapons.
The Laws of Candy.

Three others—*Wit without Money*, *The Custom of the Country,* and *Bonduca*—he is disposed to add to the above list, but with less confidence. The other plays, in number about thirty-nine, published under their joint names, he would assign either to Fletcher alone, or to Fletcher assisted by some other dramatist, not Beaumont. [The work, considerable in amount, which has been done on Beaumont and Fletcher since Dyce's day, and in which Mr. Fleay, with his metrical tests, has taken an important part, is summarized and critically sifted by Dr. A.W. Ward, in the important and elaborate chapter on 'Beaumont and Fletcher' at the end of the second volume (revised edition, 1899) of his *History of English Dramatic Literature*, pp. 643-764. Dyce's list, as given above, is still generally accepted, with the exception that the *Little French Lawyer* is now usually assigned to Fletcher and Massinger (Ward, 720); that *Wit without Money* is to be ascribed to 'Fletcher alone' (Ward, 695); that the *Custom of the Country* is probably Fletcher's only (Ward, 721); and that *Bonduca* is 'now generally regarded as Fletcher's unassisted work' (Ward, 696). The reader may also be referred to Prof. Ashely M. Thorndike's essay on 'The Influence of Beaumont and Fletcher on Shakespeare' (Worcester, Mass., 1901), as well as to Mr. Swinburne's essay on 'Beaumont and Fletcher' in his *Studies in Prose and Poetry* (pp. 53-83), the latter an attempt to distinguish the two poets and to assign to each on purely aesthetic grounds the share properly belonging to him.]

12. [Jonson's *New Inn* and *Tale of a Tub*. J.A. Symonds (*Ben Jonson*, p. 167) adds *Staple of News* and *Magnetic Lady*. Perhaps this is unjust to the last named, which, according to Langbaine, was generally accounted an excellent play; and as to the *Staple of News*, Dr. Ward writes to me that 'in conception at least it is one of Jonson's most characteristic comedies, and much superior to the *Magnetic Lady*.']

55. 12. The *Discoveries*, not published till after Jonson's death, are like the contents of a commonplace book, and of unequal merit; here occurs the well-known criticism on Shakespeare as having 'never blotted out a line.' The praise which Dryden gives to the book is perhaps excessive, though not warmer than that given by Mr. Swinburne (*A Study of Ben Jonson*).

16. *Epicoene, or the Silent Woman*, appeared in 1609.

56. 18. [The verb to 'instance' means to choose or adduce an example. In his Dictionary Johnson quotes from Tillotson:—'As to false citations... I shall instance in two or three about which he makes the loudest clamour'; and from Dryden (*A Discourse concerning the Original and Progress of Satire*, ii. 26):—'In Tragedy and Satire.... this age and the last have excelled the ancients in both those kinds; and I would instance in Shakespeare of the former, in your Lordship (Dorset) of the latter sort.' It is curious that when Johnson came to write Dorset's Life he should have forgotten his own quotation and changed the construction of the verb:—'If such a man attemped poetry, we cannot wonder that his works were praised. Dryden.... undertaking to produce authors of our own country superior to those of antiquity, says, *I would instance your lordship in satire, and Shakespeare in tragedy*.' There is yet another example of the word in Dryden's

prose (*Dedication of the Æneis*, ii. 161):—'I forbear to instance in many things which the stage cannot, or ought not to represent.' Reference should also be made to this *Essay, supra* p. 27. l. 3:— 'This is so plain that I need not instance to you that,' &c. The verb is generally followed by 'in,' and at first sight one is tempted to construe the 'in' as belonging to the verb, the verbal phrase being thus comparable to 'count in,' 'take in,' 'shut in,' and when Butler (*Analogy*, i. 6. 353) wrote, 'which is the fallacy instanced in by the ancients,' he clearly did so. But the other examples cited in the *New English Dictionary*, ranging from 1601 to 1882, prove 'in' to be an ordinary preposition. The verb can be, and has been, used without the 'in.'

57. 11. ἦθος, dispostion; πα'θος, passion (ëthos, pathos); cf. p. 112.

17. *Ex homine*. 'Terence, *Eun*. iii. 2. 7. "The one is the born image of the other"; Parmeno's remark on Gnatho the parasite and his patron Thraso' (Ker).

58. 28. Hor. *Epist*. ii. I. 168.

32. ['One of these advantages is that which Corneille has laid down as the greatest which can arrive to any poem,' &c. See Corneille's *Discours des Trois Unités*, p. 116:—'Je ne puis oublier que c'est un grand ornement pour un poëme que le choix d'un jour illustre et attendu depuit quelque temps. Il ne s'en présente pas toujours des occasions; et dans tout ce que j'ai fait jusqu'ici, vous n'en trouverez de cette nature que quatre: celui d'*Horace*, où deux peuples devaient décider de leur empire par une bataille, celui de *Rodagune, d'Andromède*, et de *Don Sanche*... dans le reste de mes ouvrages je n'ai pu choisir des jours remarquables que par ce que le hasard y fait arriver, et non pas par l'emploi où l'ordre public les ait destinés de longue main.']

59. 16. The prose comedy of *Bartholomew Fair* was produced in 1614.

60. 5. Of the piece on which our author has given so high an encomium, Drummond of Hawthornden, Jonson's contemporary and friend, has left the following anecdote: 'When his play of

The Silent Woman was first acted, there were found verses after on the stage against him, concluding that the play was well named *The Silent Woman*, because there was never one man to say *plaudite* to it' (Malone). [J.A. Symonds (*Ben Jonson*, 88) ranks the play among Ben Jonson's 'masterpieces,' though he says that, 'like all of Jonson's works, *The Silent Woman* illustrates the constructive ability of its author rather that the laws of artistic growth from within. We can see how it has been put together. We do not watch it expanding and spreading fantastic boughs like a comedy of Aristophanes. Yet the architecture is so flawless that the connection of each part seems to be inevitable.... Though so artfully constructed, *Epicoene* rather deserves the name of a Titanic farce than of a just comedy. It does not, like *Volpone*, exhibit a ruling vice, but expose a ludicrous personal peculiarity in the main actor.... But it stirs genial mirth in an ever-increasing degree; and the manners and conversation of the persons in this play, especially of the young men, are both more natural and more entertaining than is common with Jonson.' 'Its merits,' writes Swinburne (*A Study of Ben Jonson*, 50), 'are salient and superb.... this most imperial and elaborate of all farces. His wit is wonderful—admirable, laughable, laudable—it is not in the fullest and the deepest sense delightful, it is radically cruel, contemptuous, intolerant; the sneer of the superior person—Dauphine or Clerimont—is always ready to pass into a snarl.... Perhaps the only play of Jonson's which will keep the reader or spectator for whole scenes together in an inward riot or an open passion of subdued or unrepressed laughter.']

30. Hor. *de Arte Poet*. 90.

61. 4. Vell. Paterc. ii. 36.

62. 11. Macrob. *Saturnalia*, ii. 7. The 'other poet' was Publilius Syrus. [There is a fine translation of Laberius' indignant Prologue by Goldsmith (Globe edition, p. 679). The 'mime' was a scurrilous, often indecent, representation of low life, and it was an indignity for a Roman knight to appear in such a piece. Of course Caesar's request was a command. 'Laberium,' says

Macrobius, 'asperae libertatis equitem Romanum Caesar quingentis millibus invitavit, ut prodiret in scaenam et ipse ageret mimos quos scriptitabat. Sed potestas non solum si invitet, sed etiam si supplicet cogit, unde se et Laberius a Caesare coactum in prologo testatur his vocibus:—

* * * *

Ego bis tricenis annis actis sine nota
Eques Romanus e Lare egressus meo
Domum revertar mimus.'

Offended by these and other liberties of speech, Caesar turned his favour to the new star, Publilius Syrus. 'Nec ullo recusante superavit omnes, in queis et Laberium. Unde Caesar adridens hoc modo pronuntiavit:—

Favente tibi victus, Laberi, a Syro.']

26. [Aristotle's *Poetics*, iv.14, thus Englished by Professor Butcher:— 'Once dialogue had come in, Nature herself discovered the appropriate measure. For the iambic is, of all measures, the most colloquial: we see it in the fact that conversational speech runs into iambic form more frequently than into any other kind of verse; rarely into hexameters, and only when we drop the colloquial intonation.' What Aristotle says of the tendency of Greek prose to run into iambics applies in English to blank verse, 'into which,' says Dryden (*Epistle Dedicatory of The Rival Ladies*), 'the English tongue so naturally slides that, in writing prose, it is hardly to be avoided' (i. 6).] There is a curious instance in this *Essay* (p. 4, last four lines of paragraph ending 'fighting men').]

63. 9. ['Nicking.' The *Century Dictionary* gives a number of fairly apt quotations to illustrate the use of this obsolete or obsolescent word; but it is now most frequently used—and in the precise sense of the text—by the riders of tandem cycles to express the very exact correspondence between the two riders which makes the whole difference between success and failure, ease and discomfort, in that kind of cycling.]

13. Virg. *Ecl.* vii. 4.

14. Ovid, *Trist.* iv. 10. 25:—

> Sponte sua carmen numeros veniebat ad aptos,
> Et quod temptabam scribere versus erat.

30. ['Painture or designment.' Cf. Dryden's *Ode to the Memory of Mrs. Anne Killigrew*, stanza 6:

> For Painture near adjointing lay.

In the lines *To Sir Godfrey Kneller* Dryden writes:—

> As men grew polished, picture was enhanced.

Evidently Dryden was feeling about for the word 'painting,' without exaclty hitting on it. As for 'designment,' see stanza 24 of Dryden's *Oliver Cromwell*:—

> Yet still the fair designment was his own.]

64. 16. Seneca Rhetor, *Controv.* ix. 5, quoting from Ovid, *Met.* xiii. 503-5.

18. Ovid, *Met.* i. 292. This line is quoted by Lucius Seneca in *Naturales Quaest.* iii. 27. 12. [The jumble of the two Senecas, the rhetorician Marcus (? in reality we do not know his praenomen, and the M. does not appear before the fifteenth century), and the philosopher Lucius is so confusing, and the criticism, in theory and detail, so interesting, that it is worth while to quote both passages in full. First Seneca Rhetor writes (*Controv.* ix. 5. 17):—

'Habet hoc Montanus vitium: sententias suas repetendo corrumpit; dum non est contentus unam rem semel bene dicere efficit ne bene dixerit. Et propter hoc at propter alia quibus orator potest poetae similis videri solebat Scaurus Montanum inter oratores Ovidium vocare; nam et Ovidius nescit quod bene cessit relinquere. Ne multa referam quae Montaniana Scaurus vocabut, uno hoc contentus ero: cum Polyxene esset abducta, ut ad tumulum Achillis immolaretur, Hecuba dicit:—

cinis ipse sepulti
In genus hoc pugnat.
poterat hoc contentus esse; adiecit:—
tumulo quoque sensimus hostem.
nec hoc contentus est; adiecit:—
Aeacidae fecunda fui.
Aiebat autem Scaurus rem veram; non minus
magnam virtutem esse scire dicere quam scire desinere.'

Secondly, Lucius Annaeus Seneca the philosopher, in a discourse upon the Deluge (*Nat. Quaest.* iii. 27. 12), refers to Ovid's verses on the subject, and, after quoting his *montes et sparsas Cycladas augent*, goes on:—

'Ut ait ille poetarum ingeniosissimus egregie, sicut illud pro magnitudine rei dixit:—

Omnia pontus erant, deerant quoque litora ponto,

nisi tantum impetum ingenii et materiae ad pueriles ineptias reduxisset:—

Nat lupus inter oves, fulvas vehit unda leones.

Non est res satis sobria lascivire devorato orbe terrarum. Dixit ingentia et tantae confusionis imaginem cepit, cum dixit:—

Exspatiata ruunt per apertos flumina campos
. . . pressaeque labant sub gurgite turres.

Magnifice haec, si non curaverit, quid oves et lupi faciant. Natari autem in deluvio et in illa rapina protest? Aut non eodem impetu pecus, quo raptum erat, mersum erat? Concepisti imaginem quantam debebas, obrutis terris omnibus, coelo ipso in terram ruente: perfer.'

Dryden himself has said of Ovid elsewhere (*Preface to the Translation of Ovid's Epistles*, i. 234):—

'But . . . it must be acknowledged, in spite of his Dutch friends, his commentators, even of Julius Scaliger himself, that Seneca's censure will stand good against him; *Nescivit quod bens cassit relinquere*: he never knew how to give over when he had done well; but, continually varying the same sense an hundred ways, and taking up in another place what he had more than enough inculcated before, he sometimes cloys his readers instead of satisfying them.']

65.1. *The Indian Queen* and *The Indian Emperor* were the only plays, altogether in rhyme, which Dryden had produced before this was written, and *The Indian Queen* was written in part by Sir R. Howard. *The Rival Ladies* is partly prose, partly rhyme.

4. Sir Robert Howard (Malone); in the preface to his plays, published in 1665.

66. 18. 'prevail himself' se *prévaloir*, a Gallicism. See Dryden's *Preface to Annus Mirabilis* (i. 13):—'I could not prevail myself of it in the English'; and *supra*, p. 58. l. 30 (first edition). [Also *Absalom and Achitophel*, Part I, l. 461:—

> Prevail yourself of what occasion gives.

One of Dryden's few careful editors, Mr. W. D. Christie, points out that in both passages 'all the later editors, following Derrick, have printed *avail* instead of *prevail*. Dryden also uses the French idiom *to profit of*: "To profit of the battles he had won" (*Aureng-zebe*, act ii. sc i); and again to *provide oneself of*, as "Provide yourself of some more worthy heir" (*Love Triumphant, act* iv. sc.I.).' Other French words and idioms in Dryden are 'renounces to my blood' (*Hind and Panther*, 143); 'if they will criticize, they shall do it out of their own fond' (*Preface to Albion and Albanius*, i. 277); 'scabrous verse' (*Original and Progress of Satire*, ii. 70); and 'take the fraischeur of the purer air' (*Poem on the Coronation*, 102). The last of these Gallicisms is made the occasion of an attack upon Dryden's diction by Macaulay. But in point of fact Dryden is by no means a sinner in this respect. His theory is soundness itself. 'I cannot approve,' he writes

(*Defence of the Epilogue*, i. 170), 'of their way of refining, who corrupt our English idiom by mixing it too much with French: that is a sophistication of language, not an improvement of it; a turning English into French, rather that a refining of English by French. We meet daily with those fops who value themselves on their travelling and pretend they cannot express their meaning in English because they would put off to us some French phrase of the last edition; without considering that, for aught they know, we have a better of our own. But these are not the men who are to refine us; their talent is to prescribe fashions, not words.' Elsewhere (*Dedication of the Æneis*, ii. 234) Dryden has a very interesting defence of himself against the charge 'that I latinize too much.' 'When,' he says, 'I find an English word significant and sounding, I neither borrow from the Latin, nor any other language; but when I want at home, I must seek abroad... We have enough in England to supply our necessity; but, if we will have things of magnificence and splendour, we must get them by commerce. Poetry requires ornament; and that is not to be had from our old Teuton monosyllabes[1]: therefore, if I find any elegant word in a classic author, I propose it to be naturalized by using it myself; and if the public approves of it, the bill passes. . . Upon the whole matter a poet must first be certain that the word he would introduce is beautiful in the Latin, and is to consider, in the next place, whether it will agree with the English idiom: after this, he ought to take the opinion of judicious friends, such as are learned in both languages; and lastly, since no man is infallible, let him use this licence very sparingly; for it too many foreign words are poured in upon us, it looks as if they were designed

---

[1] From a German point of view the excess of monosyllables in English is a British, not a Teutonic, peculirity. Here is a characteristic fling from the England-hating Treitschke at the idea of an English-speaking world:—'So soll denn die vielgestaltige Herrlichleit der Weltgeschichte, die einst mit dem Reiche der monosyllabischen Chinesen begann, nach einem trostlosen Kreislaufe mit dem Reiche der monosyllabischen Briten endigen!' (*Deutsche Kämpfe*, ii. 351).]

not to assist the natives, but to conquer them.' And, speaking generally, Dryden's practice did not lag behind his theory. Johnson is, in this respect as in others, unjust to Dryden when he writes that 'he had a vanity unworthy of his abilities to show, as may be suspected the rank of the company with whom he lived, by the use of French words which had then crept into conversation; such as *fraîcheur* for *coolness, fougue* for *turbulence*, and a few more, none of which the language has incorporated or retained.' But even Johnson has said elsewhere of Dryden that 'to him we owe. . . the refinement of our language.' Horne Tooke said that 'Dryden's practical knowledge of English was beyond all others, exquisite and wonderful'; and Charles James Fox told Lord Holland that he would admit no word into his history, for which he had not the authority of Dryden (Christie).]

67. 20. 'Vide Daniel, his *Defence of Rhyme*.' (Dryden's note). This admirable piece of English prose was written by Daniel in 1603, in reply to Campion's *Observations in the Art of English Poesie*. It is reprinted in the third volume of Grosart's *Complete Works of Samuel Daniel* (1896).

68. 6. *The Siege of Rhodes* (1656) was one of the plays produced by Sir William Davenant under the Protectorate; 'a kind of nondescript *entertainments*, as they were called, which were dramatic in everything but the names and form; and some of them were called operas' (Hazlitt). Dryden elaborated it and added a second part in 1662.

12. ['Sometimes even to hexameter.' Speaking of the odes in Aeschylus' *Agamemnon*, Prof. Jebb discerns in them 'an epic tone, Homeric in its nobleness, and accordant with the hexameter rhythms which are so largely used' (*Classical Greek Poetry*, p. 194).]

15. 'Dryden seems not to have known any of the regular Italian tragedies in blank verse (*versi sciolti*); it is strange that he should have neglected the blank verse of Tasso's *Aminta*' (Ker).

69. 22. Virg. *Georg*. iii. 9; for *possum* should be read *possim*.

70. 3. Geo. Sandys, son of an archbishop of York, published a metrical version of the Psalms in 1636. In his *Preface to the Fables* (1700) Dryden calls him 'the ingenious and learned Sandys, the best versifier of the former age; If I may properly call it by that name, which was the former part of this concluding century' (ii. 247). His principal achievement was his translation of the *Metamorphoses*, a book much loved and read by the youthful Keats.

6. Our author here again has quoted from memory. Horace's line is [*Epist.* ii.I. 63]:—

Interdum vulgus rectum videt; est ubi peccat.

(Malone.)

12. *Mustapha* was a tragedy of the day (hissed off the stage, according to Pepys) by Roger Boyle, Earl of Orrery. There was an earlier play of the same name by Fulke Greville, afterwards Lord Brooke.

71. 4. Hor. *A. P.* 90; and below, *ib.* 231.

6. ['An ordinary sonnet.' For sonnet in the sense of any short poem see Dryden, *Dedication of the Æneis* (ii. 219):—'The genius of their (French) poets is more proper for sonnets, madrigals, and elegies than heroic poetry'; Sidney, *Apologie* (p. 53, Arber):—'They say the Lyric is larded with passionate sonnets'; and *ibid.* p. 67:—'That lyrical kind of songs and sonnets.']

11. [Aristotle (*Poetics*, xxvi. 4) argues that tragedy is superior (κρείττων) 'because it has all the epic elements—it may even use the epic metre—with the music and scenic effects as important accessories; and these afford the most vivid combination of pleasures. Further, it has vividness of impression in reading as well as in representation. Moreover, the art attains its end within narrower limits; for the concentrated effect is more pleasurable than one which is spread over a long time and so diluted... Once more, the epic imitation has less unity; as is shown by this,—that any epic poem will furnish subjects for several tragedies' (Butcher).]

72. 30 Pictoribus atuqe poetis
Quidlibet audendi semper fuit aequa potestas.

32. [Nobis non licet esse tam disertis,
Qui Musas colimus severiores.—Martial, .

Cf. Dryden's *Author's Apology for Heroic Poetry and Poetic Licence* (i. 188-9):—

'Poetic Licence I take to be the liberty which poets have assumed to themselves, in all ages, of speaking things in verse, which are beyond the severity of prose. . . . How far these liberties are to be extended, I will not presume to determine here, since Horace does not. But it is certain that they are to be varied according to the language and age in which an author writes. That which would be allowed to a Grecian poet, Martial tells us, would not be suffered in a Roman. And 'tis evident that the English does more nearly follow the strictness of the latter than the freedom of the former.'

In the Dedication to his *Examen Poeticum* (ii. 11), Dryden, agruing for what he calls synalæpha, that is, against hiatus, in verse, writes:—

'The French and the Italians have made it an inviolable precept in their versification; therein following the severe example of the Latin poets. Our countrymen have not yet reformed their poetry so far, but content themselves with following the licentious practice of the Greeks; who, though they sometimes use synalœphas, yet make no difficulty, very often, to sound one vowel upon another ; as Homer does in the very first line of the *Iliad*.... But it becomes us, for the sake of euphony, rather *Musas colere severiores*, with the Romans, than to give into the looseness of the Grecians.'

In his *Dedication of the Æneis* (ii. 217) Dryden once more recurs to this favourite quotation:—

'Virgil thinks it sometimes a beauty to imitate the licence of the Greeks, and leave two vowels opening on each other, as in that verse of the third *Pastoral*:—

Et succus pecori, et lac subducitur agnis.

But *nobis non licet esse tam disertis*, at least if we study to refine our numbers.'

Finally, Rapin (of whom Dryden says in the same *Apology* that he 'is alone sufficient, were all other critics lost, to teach anew the rules of writing'), in his *Comparaison d'Homère et de Virgile*, i. 36-37, of the edition of 1684, has the following:—

'Les transitions, qui doivent par leur caractère être fort variées, pour désennuyer la lecture, sont toutes semblables dans la plus grande partie de son ouvrage. On n'en pent compter tout au plus que de vingt ou trente sortes dans toute Pétendue to prés de trente mille vers; et ainsi une même liaison se présentant d'ordinaire est fort sujette à donner du dégoût par une si fréquente répédition; ce qui a donné même sujet à Martial de railler un peu du τὸν δ' ἀπαμειβόμενος, et de dire que les Muses latines ne sont pas tout à fait si relâchées ni si libres que les grecques: *Qui Musas colimus severiores*.'

The instances which Martial gives of the laxity of Greek poets are (1) the way in which they make Earinos (the name of a favourite of Domitian) possible for verse by spelling it Eiarinos, and (2) the use of two successive words with a different quantity for the initial syllable in each (Ἆρες Ἄρες). Of course there is a sense in which Ovid is a stricter versifier than Propertius or even than Virgil (Lucian Müller, *Res metrica*, p. 522, ed. of 1894), and Martial no doubt meant that. But when he wrote 'severiores,' the man about town may have had his tongue in his cheek, and perhaps a touch of παρα' προσδοκίαν was intended in the phrase. It is noteworthy, however, that even so serious a person as the elder Seneca (*Controv*. x. 4. 33, p. 501 of Kiessling) puts in much the same claim for Latin against Greek:— 'Graecas sententias in hoc refero ut possitis aestimare, primum quam facilis e Graeca eloquentia in Latinam transitus sit et quam omne quod bene dici potest commune omnibus gentibus sit, deinde ut ingenia ingeniis conferatis et cogitetis *Latinam linguam facultatis non minus habere, licentiae minus*.']

74. 11. The Water-poet, John Taylor, was so called from his having been long a waterman on the Thames. Wood gives an

account of him in the Athenae, and Hazlitt devotes rather a lengthy article to him in his edition of Johnson's *Lives*. Taylor enjoyed a great popularity. 'If it were put to the question,' says Ben Jonson (*Discoveries*, chap. 63, p. 34 (Dent), 'of the Water-rhymer's works against Spenser's, I doubt not but they would find more suffrages; because the most favour common vices, out of a prerogative the vulgar have to lose their judgments, and like that which is naught.'

15. Cicero in his Brutus (cap. 73) quotes this as a maxim laid down by Caesar in his work 'on the method of speaking in Latin,' to which the name 'De Analogia' was given.

20. Seneca's tragedy of *Hippolytus*, l. 863.

75. 4. The reference is to Dryden's preface to *The Rival Ladies*.

25. Sir Robert Howard, in the Preface to his Plays, before referred to.

77. 6. 'Somerset House,' says Strype in his edition (1720) of Stow's *History of London*, 'hath been used as the Palace or Court of the Queen Dowagers; it belong'd of late to Katharine Queen Dowager, the wife of King Charles the Second. At the entrance into this Court out of the Strand is a spacious square court garnished on all sides with rows of freestone buildings, and at the Front is a *Piazza*, with stone Pillars which support the buildings, and a pavement of freestone.' He goes on to say that there were steps down to the river, and a 'most pleasant garden which runs to the water side.' This way from the river bank up into Somerset House has long been closed, but in Knight's *London* there is a view of the river side of the old building, which cannot have been so near the river as the present Georgian one. Among Cowley's *Verses written on Several Occasions* is a poem in heroic couplets 'On the Queen's repairing Somerset House,' in which the poet gives Catherine of Braganza great credit for making good the ruin left by the Civil War.

80. 4. Dimock. The hereditary Champion of England, as lord of the manor of Scrivelsby. [In a letter to the *Spectator* (Feb.

23, 1901) advocating the retention or revival of the 'Services of Grand Serjeantry,' Mr. L. W. Vernon Harcourt writes:—

'The service of *King's Champion* belongs to the Dymoke family, the representative of the ancient house of Marmion, and it appertains to the manor of Scrivelsby. Documentary evidence of this service dates back to 20 Edward I; but tradition makes it a Norman service. The earliest account of the ceremony is given by a chronicler of Richard II's coronation. The great estates of the Marmions had then become dispersed. Tanfield was in the hands of the Fitz-Hughes, Tamworth belonged to Baldwin Freville, while Scrivelsby had come to the Dymokes. Accordingly, several claimants for the service presented themselves, but the Court of Claims decided for Scrivelsby. The following is a typical description of the ceremony; the scene is laid at Henry VIII's coronation feast:—

"The second course being served, in at the hall door entered a Knight armed at all points, his herald of arms before him, and presented himself to the King. This was Sir Robert Dymoke, champion to the King by tenure of his inheritance. Garter King of Heralds accosts him: 'Sir Knight, from whence came you and what is your pretence?' [After further preliminaries] his herald cries, 'Oyes'; and then proclaims:—'If there be any person, of what estate or degree soever he be, that will say or prove that King Henry VIII is not the rightful inheritor and king of the realm, I, Sir Robert Dymoke, here his champion, offer my glove to fight in his quarrel to the outraunce.' "

The proceedings terminate by the King drinking to the Champion's health out of a gold bowl, which the knight carries away with him. At the coronation of George IV the service was performed by deputy, the then lord of the manor being in Holy orders.']

10. [See Spartianus, *Vita Hadriani*, 15:—'Et Favorinus quidem, cum verbum eius quondam ab Hadriano reprehensum esset atque ille cessisset, arguentibus amicis quod idonei auctores usurpassent, risum iucundissimum movit. Ait enim, "Non recte suadetis, familiares, qui non patimini me illum doctiorem omnibus credere qui habet triginta legiones." ']

82. 5 ['For delight is the chief, if not the only, end of poesie.'

Cf. *supra*, p. 26, l. 22:—'They have ill satisfied one intention of a play, which was delight.' To quote Prof. Jebb again (*ibid.* p. 258):—'The prevalent view of the Elizabethan age, as given by Sir Philip Sidney in his *Apology for Poetry*, was that the end of poetry is 'delightful teaching.' Dryden was something of a heretic when he ventured to say, 'I am satisfied if verse cause delight, for delight is the chief, if not the only, end of poesy.' It may seem strange that the view of poetry as primarily didactic, a view which might be deemed prosaic, should have been that which was generally held by the Greeks, the most artistic of all races, in the age when their artistic faculties were at the best. But... what it really signifies, in its old Greek form, is that poetry was interwoven with the whole texture of Greek life. . .when the Greeks spoke of the poet as teacher, and of poetry as didactic, this did not imply any indifference to beauty and form, or to the delights which such form gives; it was simply a recognition of poetry as the highest influence, intellectual and spiritual, which they knew.' To be just to Dryden, it should be added that in his *Defence of the Essay* (p. 89, l. 7) he insists that 'moral truth is the mistress of the poet, as much as of the philosopher.']

34. Hor. *A.P.* 362.

83. *2. Ib* 50.

12. 'lazar' sometimes='lazar-house'; and the reference seems to be to Bartholomew's Hospital, which is the scene of the play of *Bartholomew Fair*.

84. 13. ['My conversation.' See Johnson's *Life of Dryden*:—'Congreve represents him as ready to advise and instruct; but there is reason to believe that his communication was rather useful than entertaining. He declares of himself that he was saturnine, and not one of those whose sprightly saying diverted company; and one of his censurers makes him say,—

> Nor wine nor love could ever see me gay;
> To writing bred, I knew not what to say.

...Of Dryden's sluggishness in conversation it is vain to search or to guess the cause. He certainly wanted neither sentiments nor language: his intellectual treasures were great, though they were locked up from his own use. "His thoughts," when he wrote, "flowed in upon him so fast, that his only care was which to choose, and which to reject." Such rapidity of composition naturally promises a flow of talk; yet we must be content to believe what an enemy says of him, when he likewise says it of himself.']

85. 19. ['Barach' in Hebrew means *bless*, with the antithetical meaning of *curse*, the idea being that the blessing was overdone, and so really a curse, as in vulgar English as well as in the Semitic cognates. See Driver's *Gesenius* (1893), with reference to I Kings xxi. 10, 13; Job i. 5, II, and ii. 5, 9; and Psalm x. 3. See especially Psalm x. 3 and Job ii. 9. In the former passage the Authorized Version reads:—'For the wicked... blesseth the covetous whom the Lord abhorreth,' while the Revised Version has:—'And the covetous renounceth, yea contemneth the Lord,' and in the margin suggests as an alternative:—'Or *blesseth* the *covetous*, but *contemneth*,' &c. In Job ii. 9 the famous 'curse God and die,' becomes in the Revised Version 'Renounce God and die.']

87. 7. Lucan, *Phars*. i. 12:—

> Bella geri placuit, nullos habitura triumphos.

88. 1. ['Satyr.' So spelled here by Dryden, and even throughout his *Original and Progress of Satire* (1693). But a passage from the latter essay shows that he had perceived his error:—'In the criticism of spelling, it ought to be with *i*, and not with *y*, to distinguish it true derivation from *satura*, not from *satyrus*. And if this be so, then it is false spelled throughout this book, for here it is written *Satyr*: which having not considered at the first, I thought it not worth correcting afterwards.']

9. [Malone's suggestion of Lord Lauderdale (of the Cabal) is no doubt correct; but the precise interpretation of the passage remains obscure. All we know is that about the time these words were written (1668) Lauderdale was making himself notorious

for profligacy and gormandizing. At the end of his preface to the second volume of the *Lauderdale Papers*, edited by him for the Camden Society, Mr. Osmund Airy thus sums up Lauderdale's six years of power from 1667 to 1673:—

> 'We leave him, no longer the "good Maitland," the "gracious youth" of Baillie's affection, bearing on his face, as we see it in a picture by an unknown hand, a frank intelligence and the possibilities of a noble life; but rather such as he had become when there fell upon him the solemn and sorrowful rebuke of his old friend Richard Baxter, such as we see him in Lely's well-known portrait, the type of all that was coarsest and most brutal among the men of Charles's Court; swollen with gluttony, and brutalized with vice, he bears on lip and brow the secure and shameless arrogance which befits the irresponsible proconsul of a distant province, and the privileged comrade in the pleasures of a degraded king.'

Baxter's letter, which in substance charges Lauderdale with drunkenness and vice, is given by Mr. Airy in an appendix to this volume, p. 235.]

89. 11. Hor. *de Art. Poet.* 338.

19. Sir John Birkenhead (1616-1679) in a poem, *In Memory of Mr. Cartwright*, wrote that his friend—

> Knew the right mark of things, saw how to choose,
> (For the great Wit's great work is to *Refuse*).

(Ker.)

90. 4. *Il.* viii. 267.

92. 13 See above, p. 6.

94. 6. ['Herculean'=overwhelming, knock-down. 'You have knocked him down with a kind of Herculean Club' (Howell, 1645). 'The first, which is the main and Herculean Argument' (Power, 1664—both from *New English Dictionary*). Seneca, *Epist.* 83. 23 'ille Herculaneus ac fatalis scyphus'; 87. 38 'Bonum animum habe; unus tibi nodus, sed Herculaneus restat.']